MW00937345

Karissa Block

Whoops
I Cut My Thumb Off!

I Fought the Saw and the Saw Won.

This book is dedicated to my parents,
for always encouraging me to pursue my curiosities.

Contents

Whoops
I Cut My Thumb Off!

Hello readers.

This is a story I wrote about actual experiences of my life that I recollected through my memory, my diaries and conversations with my peeps.

I did not fabricate any characters or situations, but I did change many names of people, places, and events in order to respect the privacy of parties mentioned.

Some dialogue is not exact, but it's pretty dang close… for the most part.

Some parts get a little gory.

Read at your own risk.

F&*k

Is that a thumb on the ground? I faintly remember wondering to myself. *Oh shit! Is that* my *thumb on the ground?*

It didn't take me more than a split second to realize what may have just occurred. I quickly turned around to my boss, who was standing just a few feet behind me, and I remember saying in an eerily calm voice, "I think I just cut myself. Look at my hand. Did I cut my thumb off?"

The look in his eyes answered my question before he could utter any words out of his mouth. His eyeballs grew large, and a look of dumbfounded shock covered his face. I didn't feel any pain, and surprisingly, I was completely conscious and of sound mind. I knew I had just done something major, but it would be weeks until I would truly realize that, yup, I had textbook amputated my left thumb.

"Yeah, you cut yourself good," George said to me with great concern. His voice had a tone of compassion, yet it was lined with panic.

George had a definite country boy accent, and although he was an incredibly smart man, his backwoods-type vernacular suited his role as owner of a slaughterhouse in a rural small town just outside of Lafayette, Ohio.

"Call the squad!" he shouted to whoever was listening.

There were only about four or five of us working at Lee's slaughterhouse on that busy Tuesday morning. It was the sixth of December, not even noon, when the accident occurred. The next few minutes of my life felt like hours. My thoughts were flooded with terror, each passing second longer than the last.

To be honest, I hadn't even wanted to go to work that day, even though I enjoyed my job. I had been a butcher for over a year at that point, though I should probably note the term butcher isn't always used in the professional meat world; some prefer the proper term meat-cutter. I, though, was a butcher. I butchered meat. And most days, I loved it. I loved the process of breaking hogs and beef, but I'd be lying if I didn't say the alluring magic of my newfound profession had worn off. Some days I would rather have just slept in. But who wouldn't?

That day had just so happened to be one of those days.

My absolute love for and ability to sleep is a part of my nature that those who know me either envy or despise because I can sleep anywhere, anytime, and almost on command. It has also proven to be a downfall because of the inconsistency in my ability to maintain early morning commitments.

(Insert smiley face.) What can ya do?

At the time, I lived about forty-five minutes away from the slaughterhouse. I lived in the country, and I enjoyed the beautiful early morning commute through a part of the Midwest I had grown to love. I also had another job in the city of Columbus, so living equidistant between the two fit my life seemingly well.

In Columbus, Ohio, I worked part-time at a fancy steakhouse named Smith and Wollensky. I mainly worked as a server or bartender, but I also helped the in-house butcher from time to time. Although it was also a trek to this job, I loved working there. Often times, I would work well after midnight, and it's safe to say these late nights didn't quite complement the early morning slaughterhouse schedule. Lucky for me, George would let me come in later, and often times, he would even give me the day off.

George was a wonderful man, humble to the core, and had a soft spot for this young, blonde female who loved cutting up animals as much as he did. George was a second-generation butcher and a very smart man, and he took well to the fact that I thrived on learning. He shared—and overshared—with me tons of information and stories of experience. Who would have known I would care so much for such a topic? But I did, and as I came to develop my skills as a butcher, I began to realize how fortunate I was to have had such a wonderful boss and mentor from whom I could learn more about the meat business.

Though it is to George's credit that my interest and skill set grew, if I'm being honest, I'd have to admit my passion for processing animals stemmed from my love of food, really. And George shared that love for food, meaning when we dined together, we ate well, that's for sure.

"Hold my arm up!" I nearly screamed as I leaned into his soft, red, checkered flannel shirt.

George wasn't much taller than me, and he had enough meat on his plump, well-rounded girth to keep us both warm as we stood in the 36-degree meat processing room at the back of the slaughterhouse. Usually, I'd be back there cutting and wrapping meat by myself, blaring the local country station, and enjoying the oddly pleasureful task I'd often refer to as "playing with my meats." This particular day was a Tuesday, the day we would process pork, and when the incident occurred, I was cutting up a twelve-pound pork shoulder into four three-pound roasts. I'll never forget it.

The slaughterhouse itself was not very big, as one might imagine. George owned it and inherited it from his father, who inherited it from a man with the last name Lee, hence the name Lee's Packing. George's father had worked there forty years, and George himself had worked there since he was in his twenties. He was in his late fifties when I met him, so he really knew the business inside and out. His children and the shop's manager, Howie, who was like a son to him, also grew up in the business.

I could give you a rough square footage estimate of the place, but all in all, it was no bigger than your average fast-food joint. A Panera would probably be bigger than this place, not including the holding facilities in the back for the animals, the old barn across the paved drive where they salted the hides, or the smokehouse in the basement where they smoked the ham, bacon, dog treats, and other homemade goods of country deliciousness. There was nothing tastier than slicing a sliver of freshly smoked pork side as it came out of that smoker. I could try to describe in better detail, the orgasmic feeling that came over my tongue the first time I tried it, but I'll leave that salty goodness to your imagination.

Anyway, let's get back on track here. Overall, the entire slaughterhouse was a couple thousand square feet, but I would like to paint the image of the rather small processing room we stood in—George holding my bloody, elevated arm as Howie and the other guys courageously did what they could to care for my traumatic wound.

"Somebody put my thumb on ice! Pick it up! Put it on ice!" I didn't know who was listening, but I saw Howie walk over to the corner of the room where I'd seen my thumb just moments earlier.

That image haunted me for months. I would wake up to nightmares of that eerie thought, a part of my own body detached and on the floor. The memory would flash over my eyes when I was driving, or in a yoga class, or while lying in bed watching a movie, or while out to dinner with a friend, or in the shower. Oh, how the brain works—a marvelous tool and a powerful weapon for fear.

I do, however, find it a little comical and incredibly useful how I came to know to put my thumb on ice. And I am still bewildered and grateful for my graceful presence of mind I carried throughout the whole ordeal. Granted, I was in shock, no doubt, but I was completely aware of just about everything that was happening. You see, being a 90s child, I grew up watching the TV show *Friends*. As a young adult, I had acquired all ten seasons of the TV series, and I had watched all of them multiple times. The show, if you haven't seen it, was a comedy about a group of friends and their many experiences over the course of those ten years.

In one episode, the story flashed back to when the main characters were teenagers. In a particular scene, one of the characters, Monica, a clumsy, previously overweight, nervous girl was trying to impress her older brother's college friend, and she assumed the advice of her more experienced, flirtatious friend. In the scene, Monica accidentally drops a kitchen knife through the shoe of her hoped-to-be swain, Chandler, and, as a result, severed his toe. They rushed him to the hospital where a doctor asked if they brought his toe. Though Monica believed she had brought it on ice, hoping to preserve it, it turned out she had actually brought a small piece of carrot.

Hysterical, right? I agree. So, having seen that episode enough times in my life, I remembered in those very moments after severing my own thumb on a Hobart band saw that it would be in my best interest to immediately put my thumb on ice. Thankfully, though, I was not the person to actually pick it up and there were no small carrots in sight to confuse anyone. (Howie, I love you forever for your bravery.) I suppose when you deal with meat and bones all day it might not be that big of a deal, but there's something about picking up your own meat and bones that seemed a little traumatizing.

I do not do well with gore, which might sound rather hypocritical due to the fact that I worked at a slaughterhouse and literally loved the process of turning live animals into tasty food morsels. However, when it comes to humans and suffering and nasty wounds—bleh! Count me out. I could never be in the medical field despite my mother's hopes that I would follow in her footsteps.

"Can you put pressure on my hand to stop the bleeding?" I hesitantly asked as the initial shock started to wear off and I began to feel faint. Somehow, I was still bossing others around, even though I was rather unsure of who was listening and tending to my care at this point.

"It's not bleeding, sweetie," George replied, sounding a little shocked.

I was confused. *Wouldn't blood be spurting out like in the movies?*

"It's gonna be okay. You're okay," he kept assuring me in a caring, fatherly tone.

I could hardly feel Howie cleaning the blood off of my hand and arm because of my state of mind. I remember thinking to myself, "So this is what shock feels like."

"She needs a chair," Ted, another valiant coworker said. "I'll bring her one," he announced with fear-soaked concern.

And he did.

I want to say it was only about ten minutes before the ambulance arrived; I know it wasn't very long. The entire time, George embraced me, comforted me, and soothed my nerves and anxieties with courageous and encouraging words. I remember drinking a few sips of Mountain Dew, and the sugary bubbles burst with ecstasy in my mouth. George was surprised I asked for a soda because I usually tote around my large pink, dirtied up, REI Nalgene water bottle, but he didn't question me. I could tell he just wanted to ease the situation in any way possible.

I clung to his shirt, the softness comforting me, and focused on his repeated words: "Everything will be okay." I could tell he was crying, so I kept apologizing. For being a surefooted burly man who owns and runs an intimidating business, he sure does have and share some deep emotions. Hell, I wasn't even crying! I was laughing, and then I was apologizing profusely as I tried to determine what the hell just happened. *Did I really just cut off my fucking thumb?*

I never looked at my hand. My subconscious was all over me, like, "Girl, don't you look at that hand! Just keep focusing on the warm, squishy flannel in front of you! You can't feel it, so you definitely don't need to see it. We're good! Let's just pretend nothing happened."

It wasn't long before I was swarmed with attention from the emergency medical responders. There seemed to now be a sea of people around me, asking questions and tending to my wounds. One uniformed gal immediately pricked my shoulder with a tiny needle that instantly calmed my growing nerves. Once I was loaded into the ambulance, Howie popped his head in. "Will you text Annie and let her know what happened?" I asked. Annie was my roommate, and I wanted her to be notified about the accident and where I'd be headed.

"I'll go ahead and give her a call," he reassured me.

"Thanks, Howie," I replied with what I hoped was sincere gratitude in my eyes. "For everything."

"Sure thing, missy," Howie, who was about as country and well-mannered as they come, said and then closed the doors.

I was secured in the ambulance, and we headed to the nearby hospital. Once I was seen and briefly evaluated at the local hospital, I was told that I needed to go to another hospital in Columbus, about forty minutes away, where the hand surgeon specialists worked. Not long after, I was transferred to another gurney and wheeled into another ambulance. It was raining hard outside, which was pretty typical for Ohio, and by this time, my system was filled with happy drugs that allowed me to not feel the pain of my injury. I think it was the combination of the drugs and the slightly sinister sense of humor the EMT, Dave, and I shared that encouraged me to take a Snapchat video while in the ambulance.

He held my thumb in a bag next to me as I informed the camera, "Alright, snappers, it happened. I cut my thumb off, and it's on Snapchat. Hah! Thanks to Dave, we're headed to the hospital."

We both laughed, and then I wearily laid back, as I tried to piece this all together. I knew what had happened, but I still didn't want to *see* it. I knew that if I looked at my hand after seeing my severed thumb on the ground, I would surely pass out. It would have made things more real, I guess. Thankfully, both my hand and my severed appendage were bandaged, and to this day, I am so glad I don't have the image of my mangled hand etched into my mind.

It took me nine days to work up the courage to even glance down at my hand.

Me

When I was eighteen years old, I got a job at a local casino in Reno, Nevada—or maybe I was seventeen. Anyway, I had a friend who worked there, and she excitedly encouraged me to apply. I had some experience working at a sandwich shop and a small Italian restaurant in my hometown of Carson City, so I applied to work in the deli of The Tamarack Junction. "Your junction for fun!" as the motto went. I called repeatedly every day after I had submitted my application to ask the human resources manager if she'd received my application. "The squeaky wheel gets the oil," my parents often said.

After finally squealing loud enough, the gal set me up to come in for an interview within the week. I was so excited, and I was in luck the day I'd arrived because the HR woman with whom I had originally spoken was out for the day, so I interviewed directly with the executive chef. Little did either of us know at the time, but this day would mark the beginning of an ever-evolving, exponentially, and mutually beneficial relationship for the next ten-plus years. In a nutshell, my life changed when I met Executive Chef Jim Reed from the Tamarack Junction (as his voicemail *still* says. I'm not kidding. It's exactly the same, even a decade later).

We sat across from one another at a boardroom table that was big enough for over twelve people. The room was quiet, and I felt intimidated as he asked me questions about my work experience and professional goals. I was nervous, but my enthusiasm seeped through my smiling face and vivacious hand gestures as I spoke. Before our time together was finished, he offered me the job upon consulting with human resources. Later, he would often reiterate how candid I was, not only in my interview but seemingly also in my life.

We became friends instantly. He was a great role model for this knowledge-hungry young woman. "The charming and lovely Miss Block," he would call me. And he actually still does to this day. I did not necessarily know it then, but throughout the first years of employment with this growing company, I realized I had a passion for food and natural talent in the kitchen.

As a teenager, I worked in a deli because I loved sandwiches. When I was a kid, I begged my dad to take me to Port of Subs like every day. This was my favorite sandwich shop where I grew up in Carson City, the capital of Nevada. I think I loved Port of Subs so much because they premixed the mayonnaise and mustard, which to me was like a mind-blowing secret sauce.

If I never touch on this topic again throughout this story, I will boldly and proudly say I have a deep-rooted passion for sauce. All sauce. Multiple sauces. I love wet, sopping, I-can-dip-anything-into-this sauce.

I used to tell the girl who managed my favorite sandwich shop that when I was old enough, I wanted to work there. I was maybe just eight years old at the time, and lo and behold, as soon as I turned fifteen, I got my dream job as a sandwich artist at Port of Subs.

Working at this deli was such a wonderful experience. First of all, I loved it, so I was enthused to go into work every day. I'd happily prepare sandwiches and just as merrily scrub the bathrooms from floor to ceiling. I gradually moved up in my shift duties and responsibilities, anxiously awaiting when I would be eighteen and old enough to use the meat slicer. I used to long for the day when I could use the sharp, powerful piece of equipment. (Ha! Isn't that funny?)

I worked there for just less than three years, and I learned a lot during those precious years. I made some friendships that helped develop me into the thrill-seeking good girl that I am, and I established myself as an employee with work history. Without those years at Port of Subs, I would never have had the suiting title on my resume as a "sandwich artist." Yes, that is precisely and proudly what I would fill in under the position inquiry space on job applications.

I was just as enthusiastic to work as a deli girl for the Tamarack Junction as I was to work as a deli girl at Port of Subs. The Tamarack Junction was a small, locals' casino, and at the time, it contained the Whistlestop Deli, Sully's Sports Bar, and the Dining Car restaurant. After about six months, I quickly mastered the deli, so I would often help with some of the main kitchen prep duties during my downtime. It wasn't long before the charming and lovely Miss Block became a full-time prep cook and also got her first pay increase. Welcome to the real world: work harder, and make more money! This was an attractive feature I learned about adulting. Due to my money-driven nature, I vowed to put in as much blood, sweat, and tears as I deemed necessary to increase my income. I would always ask what else I could do, how else could I help, and to please teach me anything and everything that could further my career and fatten my pocketbook.

I yearned for knowledge as equivocally as I yearned for cash. This quality helped me to continue to move up from prep cook, to line cook, to banquet chef, to an off-site chef, and then to a table-side chef as well as to earn the ego-stroking nickname of Super K all over the course of about four years. In total, I worked at the Tamarack for eight years and eleven months, but I tell everyone a decade. Who doesn't round up?

Aside from the encouragement from my friend, I guess my motivation to start working at the casino stemmed from an encounter, or lack thereof, I had with my dad and stepmother. Up until I was eighteen, I lived at their house. For my eighteenth birthday in March, I went to Cabo San Lucas with my best friend, Sandy. Oh, I'm so royally screwed if I ever have kids and all the shit I put my parents through comes back around. Do all parents think like this before they become parents? This alone might be reason enough to practice safe sex. Lord, do I get off track or what? If you can't handle this, I suggest you put the book down now. Where was I… Oh yes, Mexico.

When I'd returned from my first true adventure as an adult (Ha! Adult? Right.), I came home to most of my belongings packed in black trash bags on the foyer to my parents' house—an implication it was time for me to move out. Conversations around the dinner table were not really my family's forte, so I loaded up as much as I could into my big ole truck and headed to Sandy's house. Thankfully, her parents owned the home where she lived, and she let me move in promptly. Oh, that year of my life—it's thankfully a distant memory to me now, but it at least is what prompted me to spread my little wings. The casino was the perfect place for a young adult to learn about herself, her work ethic, her passions, her abilities, and what it means to appreciate responsibilities. Oh yes, and let's not forget about earning money!

Though nothing compares to the riches we see in the media or the true demographic of affluence, for living just outside of Carson City, Nevada, my family was pretty well off. My dad was an important VP of a gaming company after having developed and sold his own gaming software business, my stepmom worked as a smarty-pants head of the IT department for the attorney general, and my mother was up in the top tiers of the nursing hustle in

Carson as she'd worked her ass off her entire life to achieve success, gain pay increases, and forge a healthy retirement plan. I am thankful to come from the smart, hardworking, motivated family that I come from because those qualities oozed onto me as the sweat of a heifer might spill onto her nursing calf during a dewy midsummer's day.

The Tamarack soon became my home away from home. I worked under the watchful eye of my mentor, Jim Reed, and Jim treated me as and would even sometimes refer to me as "the daughter he'll never have." At the time, Jim was in his fifties, and he and his wife had a son, who was born only a few months after I was hired. This came to play an important factor in our relationship because I happened to have a little brother who was born just six months prior to his son. This greatly impacted the development of Jim's and my relationship because the fact that I had a little person whom I often cared for led me to also become the Reeds' nanny. How convenient that Jim could make my work schedule around his babysitting needs?

Over the years, it worked out wonderfully. I earned extra money, and their son, Junior, got an amazing babysitter—and sometimes playmate when I brought my little brother along. All the while, Jim helped to develop my experience as a chef. I loved to learn, and he explained things well. He also taught me office work and behind-the-scenes management as well as frontline cooking. The size of the company was perfect—small and family run, but big enough to have different outlets for professional creativity and personal growth.

About four to five years into my career at the casino, I had reached the maximum limit of hourly pay I could get. This was a real eye-opener for me. No matter how much I cared, no matter how many extra hours I put in, how much I cleaned, or how much I went above and beyond the call of duty, I could no longer increase the dollars per hour I made. It was a harsh truth, but over time and with adequate counseling, I learned that I would have to make some changes, or I would just be frustrated and not truly working to my potential. "You are either making money, spending money, or sleeping," I remember Guy Archer said, one of my favorite mentors at the casino.

Not long after this season where I realized the truths of the job world, a discreet job opening was presented to me. You see, in order to keep me happy, since my boss could not increase my pay, he gave me my favored schedule. I was working Monday through Friday, seven to three, as a line cook in the sports bar at the Tamarack Junction. It was my comfort shift, and it allowed me to have freedom and a life outside of work, which was the only way to remain sane in a world I was just beginning to understand as a young adult.

The opportunity was presented to me by the waitress who worked the same shift at the sports bar. She was the only waitress during those hours, so we grew to become dear friends. She was a gem of a person, beautiful in both her appearance and demeanor. She valued family, integrity, and relationships, and I admired her. She had discreetly informed me that she was pregnant and planning to leave her position. She knew my struggles with wanting more income, and she shared with me the money she made and gently reminded me that she worked about ten fewer hours per week than I did. It was hard for me to believe because I knew she made minimum wage, but she encouraged me that the clientele she served was generous and that I had the ability and personality to fill her shoes, which would not only increase my profits but also allow me more time to enjoy my personal life. Hmm...very interesting.

14

Needless to say, when I presented the idea to Jim, he was not in favor. I first went to him as a friend and mentor, and then I approached him again as a boss with some leverage. If he wanted to keep me as a line cook, he'd have to pay. He didn't want me to leave; however, he was unable to give me what I desired, so before long, I threw in my chef hat and traded it for a little black apron and a Micros key card. The transition was not instant. I actually worked my way into the position for about six months or so because, obviously, since I was not a waitress, I did not get first dibs on the Monday through Friday position. I worked the back of the house still a couple days a week and worked the front of the house the remainder of my forty-hour availability, picking up any extra hours or overtime the company would allow. My sweet little mom-to-be was right; the customers loved me, and I was able to increase my pay.

This transition turned out to be a huge stepping stone in my life. I no longer poured myself into a company hoping to find my worth in the work efforts I did not get rewarded for. I began to build relationships with people, and I found my compassion and empathy for others would open doors and increase my growth financially, personally, and relationally. I also stepped into opportunities presented to me by customers whom I served regularly. Some even networked for me, knowing my desires, skills, and talents. In this position, I met the realtors who would help me buy a house. I met various strangers who invited me into their homes and offered me opportunities to cater private events, who needed help moving furniture, and one woman who I assisted in an estate sale. These were chances for me to earn some cash, to learn, and to grow to be involved in my community. It was there, in this waitress position, that I learned there was more value in relationships than in any financial raise I could ever obtain.

Throughout these years, I continued to be close with Jim, he was certainly a father figure to me. Even though I no longer worked directly for him as a back-of-house employee, our relationship continued to blossom. He would come out to the sports bar to "contemplate life," as he would put it, during his few and far between breaks. Sometimes, I would be busy with my waitress duties, and other times, I would be belly-up at the bar as a patron myself. Regardless of when we would catch a moment to shoot the breeze, I found myself sincerely speaking to him about the goings on in my life. Having been through his own share of tribulations, he was an irreplaceable friend and fountain of wisdom for me.

It wasn't uncommon for me to find myself sitting at the bar after my shift. The casino gave employees a free drink ticket with our paychecks, and I would eagerly cash in these tasty libations regularly. The casino staff was like a family, so it was more than just having a drink after work; I was spending time with my loved ones, even if they were still working. This pastime quickly grew into a habit that left me sitting on a barstool until the late hours of the night. Other employees would, one-by-one, finish their respective shifts, and the group gradually grew until it was mainly employees filling the seats at the bar.

One night, after I had had a few too many Fireball shots and Coors Light chasers, I made the elementary decision to drive myself home. After all, it was only a twenty-minute drive, half of which could be taken on the backroads. A fellow coworker offered to follow me for a bit on the freeway, and I gleefully obliged the offer. As I exited the freeway, I noticed she continued to follow me. This gave me some sense of confidence that I would make it home safely. I made the right-hand turn off the exit ramp, and I knew it was just one more veer to the right until I would be on the home stretch.

My stomach, filled with a medley of spirits, convulsed when I saw bright red and blue lights illuminate the dark streets around me.

Oh fuck.

As I pulled onto the shoulder, I felt instantly sober. Fearful thoughts flooded my mind as I realized what was happening. I quickly rustled through my glovebox to get the paperwork I knew would be requested. I turned off the car's engine and reached to manually roll down the passenger window as I saw a vague figure approach my vehicle with a curious flashlight peering into the windows.

"Good evening," a stern voice announced. "License and registration," he stated.

As soon as the officer bent down to look at me, I noticed a slight change in the expression on his face. I knew him. I served this uniformed officer lunch regularly at the casino. It became obvious to me that he recognized me too. I handed him the documents he requested and did not say a word. He stood at the side of my car for a brief moment and then turned to walk back to his vehicle. Within seconds he returned to the passenger window of my car. My heart was racing, and my mind was frozen in the moment.

"This is your lucky day, Ms. Block," the man said as he returned my documents to me. "I have an emergency call. You get home safe."

The encounter didn't last more than five or six minutes. My thoughts scrambled to process what happened. I was in no shape to drive that night, and to be honest it was not to first, second, or third time I had chosen to get behind the wheel after drinking for hours at the bar. This occurrence surely shocked me into checking myself and my lifestyle decisions.

I had displayed some detrimental behaviors abusing alcohol for a few years at this point, and I couldn't help but feel as if this incident was a lucky break. I spent the next day imagining how I could have easily ended up in jail for driving under the influence, which led me to contemplate the direction of my life. *Was this the person I wanted to be?*

I turned to Jim for support, knowing he had overcome some similar habits to the ones I had developed. I called him before I went to work.

"Hi, Cheffie!" I announced in my normal energetic tone.

"Well if it isn't the charming and lovely Miss Block!" his familiar words warmed my heart.

"Do you have some time this morning for a cup of coffee?"

"Sure," he said, cordially welcoming the offer. "I'll brew a pot now. See you when you get here."

I arrived at the casino, and we sat in an empty booth in the dark restaurant that wasn't due to open for another hour and a half. It wasn't uncommon for us to be found conversing over a pot of coffee, but the mood of that day was certainly somber. I told him about what had happened and I that I felt frightened and guilty. He listened and understood my sentiments. He shared with me some disheartening stories of his own. And after some time, he explained to me the incentives and strategies that kept him sober.

"It will not be easy," he encouraged me, "but it will be worth it." His words charred my heart.

It was at this time that he exposed me to the lifestyle of exercise and fitness. We began to run together, expanding my world and also our relationship. I was able to forge new friendships that were laden with sobriety, focus, endorphins, and enthusiasm. Not only was Jim my mentor at work and outside of work, but he was my friend, and he wanted only to help me to continue to flourish.

When I still worked solely for him in the back of the house at the casino, amidst our array of conversations over prepping for busy nights and big parties, Jim would speak to me about his family back in Ohio. He'd explain how his mother was a passionate gardener and how they lived on a huge farm surrounded by cows and cornfields and farmers alike. He'd talk about his sister and brother-in-law and their cattle operation and how much I would be tickled by their set up, a half-mile lane that led back to their lovely home and a huge, rustic barn filled with horses and cats. He shared with me about his niece who also enjoyed running, and subsequently, he tried to convince me that she and I had similar interests and personalities. He told me that I would probably enjoy meeting all of them.

Jim knew I rode horses as a pastime and that my dad had some land outside of the city. Working side by side for so many years, he grew to know more of my passions and things that made my heart sing. I loved adventure and animals, and I loved to cook and experiment with food. My seemingly endless curiosity for understanding how things worked and where they came from always had me questioning the origin of the tasty morsels in front of me in the kitchen. From animal proteins to spices to the little curls of macaroni, I needed to know the full story: Where did this come from, how did it get to this form, and who helped get it there? Something inside of me knew there wasn't a macaroni tree, but if there were, what would it look like, and how would they harvest it? My great paternal grandmother, Ma, would say, "Curiosity killed the cat, but satisfaction brought it back!" That phrase resounded deep in my soul.

Jim and his little family would travel back to Ohio for annual visits for his father's birthday celebration in June, and for about four years, he would return and say to me, "You really ought to fly out and see the farm someday. Maybe you can come with us next year."

"Okay, yeah, sure, Cheffie. Sounds great," I would reply sarcastically, as if I would ever truly fly across the country with my boss to meet some random farm folk.

Then, one year, around February, he was planning his annual visit to Ohio in June, and he again said, "Why don't you fly out with us to Ohio this year? You can watch Junior while we spend some time with the folks. Then, we'll ship you on down to the sister's farm for a few days, and you can see them in action. Maybe ride some horses? We'll put you up and feed you, and you will only have to pay for your plane ticket. I'll talk to my niece, and maybe she can show you how the Midwestern girls have fun."

At that point, I felt stagnant in my life, and that's never been a safe place for this girl. Without really thinking about it, I found myself saying, "Okay, Cheffie. Why not?" I felt the need for adventure stirring within me, and I was looking for excitement. So, needless to say, I purchased my plane ticket to Ohio.

Timing is everything.

Daze

There was an angelic glow behind Margaret's head as she leaned over me and announced in a loving tone, "Hi, Karissa. You are just waking up from surgery."

My eyes attempted to focus on her face, and I began to recollect who I was, where I was, and what was going on. I smiled.

"Do you know where you are?" she inquired.

I nodded.

"You are at Riverside Hospital in Columbus," she encouraged me.

I nodded again.

"Do you know what happened to you?" she asked.

"I cut my thumb off," I replied, my lips hardly peeling from each other as I muttered the words.

"That's right, sweetie. Good. Yes, your surgery went very well. And do you know what year it is?"

"Two thousand…sixteen?"

"Yes, it is. Can you tell me what month it is, Karissa?"

"December. It's almost Christmas." I smiled and began to regain a little more consciousness, although I felt utterly spent.

"That's right, Karissa, and how are you feeling?" the precious woman asked.

I nodded again. "My throat hurts." My voice cracked, and I swallowed hard.

"That's because you had a tube down your throat. It is going to be a little painful to swallow, okay?" Her tone was sympathetic and calming. It was obvious this woman was wonderful at her job as a nurse in the recovery room. "Can I get you some water?"

I smiled and nodded again—those seemed to be my strongest means for communication at the time. She held a cup of water with a straw in it before my lips, and I did my best to take a sip. The shock of the cool liquid crept down my esophagus, soothing every centimeter on its way down my throat. I'm not sure if the sensation felt more painful or refreshing.

"We're going to need to keep you up here for a bit, and then we'll take you down to another room, okay?" Every word she spoke was as if she was speaking to a five-year-old. "Have you ever been in a hospital before?"

"Yes," I replied. I cleared my throat as I began to recall instances in my youth that brought me to the hospital.

"What happened to you before? Can you tell me?" she asked. It didn't occur to me at the time, but I gather she was asking me questions per protocol in order to gauge my consciousness or coherence after being under anesthesia.

"Lots of broken bones… I had my tonsils removed…and I had a bad head injury." I told her.

"A brain injury?" she asked.

I nodded.

"What happened?"

"I suffered from frontal lobe damage when I was fourteen," I announced.

"You hear that, Karen?" I remember Margaret calling out to the other recovery nurse. "This girl had a TBI when she was fourteen!"

"Wow!" Karen replied with sympathy. "She must be a tough one!"

Margaret looked back down at me and reassured me, "You're going to be just fine, honey."

Again, I smiled.

"And guess what, Karissa? Your mom is here. I am going to let her in to see you in just a few minutes, okay?" Margaret's words were like soft angel kisses to my ears. Tears began to fall out of my eyes.

"Are you doing okay?" she asked when she saw my emotion.

"Yes..." I murmured, my words choking me up a bit. "I just can't wait to see my mom."

I couldn't believe she was there, in the building. She didn't even live in the same state. *How did she get here so fast?* I wondered. I briefly tried to recall all the events of that day, but it wasn't long before I could hear my mom's voice in the distance. I began to softly sob.

"Hey, baby girl," the most familiar and relieving words rang in my ears. My soft sob turned into full-fledged tears of joy as my compassionate mother brushed her hands upon the top and sides of my face. She kissed me on the cheek.

I could see her smile radiating as she briefly exchanged some friendly medical personnel banter with the nurses. I began to rest in the arms of comfort, allowing the daze of the withering anesthesia to perform its final dance within me.

"Annie and George are downstairs, honey," my mom informed me.

More tears flowed down my cheeks, and she wiped them away.

They're still here? I thought. They had been with me all day, George from the slaughterhouse to both hospitals and sweet Annie when we first arrived at the emergency room at Riverside.

Annie, Jim's niece and a cowgirl through and through, played a crucial role in my story. Not only was she the farmer who invited me to live in her home, but she was also the steady stream of fuel that allowed me to move across the country and keep my flame lit on my journey. She made feel comfortable and welcome in the Midwest. If it weren't for her, kin to my soul, I know my life would look quite different.

"Can they come in?" I asked.

It was just moments before I saw both of their faces. We were all teary-eyed. I felt overjoyed, overwhelmed, and overtired. I imagine those feelings were shared between the whole lot of us. Concern and compassion filled the air as we all marveled in the fact that my surgery had gone over five and a half hours.

"For that little thumb," George commented as his watery eyes looked at mine. What a relief it was to see this look in his eyes compared to the panic-stricken expression I had seen on his face that morning. It wasn't long before I knew in my heart that everything was going to be okay.

"I can't believe you are still here!" I commented to both Annie and George. It was now almost midnight, and my injury had occurred before noon that day. Needless to say, it was a long day for all.

"I couldn't drive home without knowing you were okay," George said with concern.

"I figured I'd stay since I'd already taken the day off!" Annie chimed in with her slight twang and ear-to-ear smile.

She is adorable. "Thank you." I looked at each of the faces surrounding me and lay back in exhaustion.

I started to piece together the moments of my day prior to waking up in the recovery room. Annie showed up at the hospital thanks to Howie, the manager at the slaughterhouse. He called her to inform her of what happened and where I would be. Unbeknownst to me, she drove straight to Columbus as soon as she heard. She peered into the glass window on the door of the emergency room where I was placed when I first arrived at Riverside. Just the sight of her brought me instant relief. I was alone for a period of time and to have her be the first familiar face filled me with a sense of peace I didn't know I needed. She sat with me and kept the mood light, though I suppose the morphine helped with that too.

We were unsure what to expect when the doctor had originally walked into the emergency room to inspect my amputated appendage. He had partially removed the blanket from my feet and grabbed my big toe as he stated, "If the thumb doesn't take, we will have to supplant your toe to your hand."

I thought he was kidding. He wasn't. Although his words were disturbing to hear, I didn't believe him. *He's not really going to cut off my big toe, is he?*

The surgeon then moved to the corner of the room, where my thumb lay neatly packed on ice, to obtain an assessment of his surgical operation.

"I'm wiggling it now. Is it moving?" I asked the doctor in jest, hoping to relieve the airtight tension I felt building up during those lingering silent moments.

"Your thumb looks good, so I think we will be able to reattach it," he proclaimed.

He completely disregarded my joke, but perhaps he didn't hear me. Afterall, he was like seventy-five years old.

I let out a howl of happiness. That was the first moment I let myself weep since the amputation. I'd spent hours imagining what I would do without a thumb. I was probably still in shock, but for the first time that day, I was filled with hope. And I was so thankful Annie was by my side.

After the operation and my brief time in the recovery room, I was soon moved downstairs to the room I'd be staying in for the next few days. By then my mom was with me. And it was in that hospital room, in the

Intensive Care Unit, where I was covered with those deliciously warm, heated blankets. Oh my, how I loved those blankets. The team of nurses also kept my left hand under a heat lamp during my stay in order to maintain blood flow to my thumb.

It's like I have a goddamn holiday ham sitting next to me under the bright red light by my bedside, I thought to myself. *Oh wait, that's just my reattached digit keeping warm.*

Since I had a replant, it was important to keep it warm. Constriction of the artery, for any reason, would cause a lack of blood flow to my thumb and, in turn, could cause the replant to "not take." The first seventy-two hours are the most critical for this sort of injury. The nurse staff would come in hourly and check the blood flow from my thumb. During surgery, the doctor had removed my nail; he needed to stimulate bleeding at the top of my thumb in order to make sure my veins were functioning properly. One of the gals explained to me that they even sometimes use leeches in this situation to encourage blood flow; luckily, I was oozing blood at a healthy rate and did not need to go that route.

Once I was settled into my room, a team of nurses came in to check on me. They explained my surgery and a brief overview of how my immediate recovery would go. They informed me that I would be in the hospital a few days so they could make sure my thumb replant was successful. They asked if I had any questions.

"Will I be able to work over Christmas?" I asked the lead nurse.

She looked at the other two gals beside her, and they all exchanged awkward glances, as if to see which one would deliver the what seemed to be obvious news.

"I don't think you will be working for a while," one of them replied.

"Replants are usually a long recovery," another added.

This truth dumbfounded me as I still had little cognizance of the severity of my situation. "But we are extremely busy during the holidays, and my work is definitely going to need me."

"Honey," my mom chimed in with her nurturing tone, "they will survive without you. There is no way you're going back to work by then."

Finally, the harsh truth. It was a tough pill to swallow, but that was the first moment it even crossed my mind that I wouldn't be bouncing back from this right away. I mean, in all reality, I didn't even feel much pain. Sure, I could hardly move my left arm, and there was a great deal of blood and attention from the medical staff, but this wasn't my first rodeo. I figured I would get stitched up and sent on my merry way.

I let the weight of that soak in, trying to imagine what I would do with my time without work. I felt fine, my injury seemingly nonexistent. It wasn't until a few days later that I was hit with a whole new truth—pain. Initially, from surgery, I had a nerve block on my arm so I could not feel anything below my left shoulder at all for the first three days. Once they removed the block, however, it only took about four hours for me to feel, for the first time, the excruciating pain in my hand.

"Oh my Gooooddd," I repeated in agony about a thousand times that day.

I was on a pretty strict regimen of Dilaudid and Vicodin during that time. At first, they administered to me Oxycodone, but that powerful medicine gave me extreme nausea and knocked my senses into orbit. It didn't take long for the endless complaints to my mother to prompt her to inquire if they could switch me to a painkiller my body could tolerate a little better. My amazing, brave nurse of a mother was the best person to have beside me during those days.

On top of the pain from my thumb, I suffered migraines throughout my stay at the hospital. To anyone who suffers from migraines or knows anyone directly who suffers from them, you might understand how debilitating and unfortunate these ailments can be. I spent half of my time at the hospital vomiting from the migraines and painkillers and the other half with my eyes under a damp, cool cloth. My mother did her best to keep comforting and taking care of me. And to top it off, my doctor would not allow me to take my prescription migraine medicine because it is a vasoconstrictor, meaning it constricts blood flow in the veins. Since I had just had a vein reattached in my thumb, I was unable to take the medicine for fear that my thumb wouldn't take.

Oh, the anxiety, fear, and pain all felt during those dreadfully long first days left me in a daze. My friend Juke, who I befriended during the previous year in Ohio, was a solid source of support when I was in the hospital. I am so thankful for him and my mom, who took the greatest care of me. I also had other dear friends visit me in the hospital and bring me goodies and clothes, trinkets and treats. What a blessing to feel all of this support during such a tumultuous time in my life, especially since I was so far away from home.

The day I was released from Riverside, I was no longer on the hospital-strength pain relievers. I was equipped with painkillers for the coming weeks, but the instant relief of the injections into my veins would no longer be available. Enter endurance. I was beginning to learn how much this injury was going to hurt. Each agonizing step of the way could only be endured moment by moment. I had not a care in the world except if I could survive each second's misery.

Before going home, the first line of business after being wheeled from my familiar hospital room was to head to the Hand Center, which would be my home away from home for the next nine or so months. It was snowing outside. Of course, it was dreadfully cold too. After all, it was December in Ohio. I had strict orders to keep my hand warm. On top of the bandages provided, my hand was wrapped in an Ace bandage, placed into a sling, and then wrapped again with a scarf. This look was a trend I would patent over the next three weeks. I was graciously covered with a wool shawl and also the final layer of big down jacket draped over my shoulders. I was ready for transport.

We made our way to the Hand Center, which was a special facility just for hand injuries, about a twenty-minute commute from the hospital. My friend Juke, who you will hear more about later, played a tremendous role in my Ohio existence as well as throughout my entire recovery. I know we will be friends for life. He was our chauffeur that day as well as my calming tea. He was like my security blanket, and I know my mom appreciated having the help and resources found in him.

Not long after we arrived at the Hand Center, which was actually co-founded by my surgeon, the lovely staff put me in a private room as they could see the uncomfortable affliction I was experiencing. On top of it all, I was still suffering from a migraine that had been lingering for the past few days. In addition to being wrapped up like a newborn baby, I also had a soft black hat pulled down over my eyes to protect my sensitive brain from the excruciating light that beamed throughout the building. We were there to get fitted for a splint and to schedule appointments for follow-ups and physical therapy to come, but I was only in the private room for about ten minutes before the fire alarm went off.

As you could imagine, I panicked in that initial moment. Being partially blind from my migraine and wrapped up like stuffed sausage, all I could think was, "What the hell can I possibly do right now?"

Alleviating my stress, a pleasant voice popped into the room with my mother, Juke, and me and said, "You don't have to go anywhere. This is just a drill."

I was relieved and frustrated at the same time. I was relieved that I didn't have to move again after we struggled to get up to the second floor, checked in, and shuffled back to this tiny room where it took all three of us to undress me from all of my layers without further agitating my migraine or disturbing my freshly reattached thumb. And I was frustrated because there was a fire alarm drill at that very moment. Of course I would be pushed to the breaking point of tolerance. Before I could fully lose it, thankfully, an angel walked in, signifying the actual start of my healing journey.

Angela only stood about five feet off the ground. She had a gorgeous smile and a soothing, motherly way about her that made me believe her three kids were abundantly nurtured and dearly loved. She would be my physical therapist for the next year and a half. We shared similar interests and beliefs, compassion and spirit, as well as gossip and encouragement from the first moments we spent together to the last tear-filled goodbye. I told her when I was writing this book that I would refer to her as an angel because, after all, she was an angel watching over me.

That first day, Angela just suited me up in a splint and laid the initial foundation with my mother and me in an attempt to paint the picture of what this road to recovery might look like. My mom was comforted by knowing she was leaving me in good, loving hands since she could only stay to take care of me for the first two weeks.

When we finally made our way out of the Hand Center that day and down to my truck, which my mom had already started in order to warm the engine and crank the heater to ease my exposure of the brisk outdoors, we came to the painstaking realization that she'd mistakenly locked the keys inside of the running vehicle. As if we hadn't endured enough that day, we then had to sit and wait for the tow truck, which took about forty-five minutes to unlock the roaring diesel that idled in the parking lot. At this point, I let myself fall out of reality and into the coma of being cared for and drugged up because, frankly, there was nothing more I could do. And my angels surrounded me. And I had made it this far. And I was on my way home to the house I had called home for over eighteen months, tucked away from the city on a cozy, love-filled farm in the snow-covered country. And my mom was with me.

Everything was going to be okay.

Pursuit

Sometimes, life just works out the way it's supposed to. Sometimes, you can navigate and orchestrate events and plan for anticipated, intentional moves. Other times, life will unleash plot twists and unveil opportunities beyond your current imagination. In this particular case, I had already purchased my plane ticket to go to Ohio with Jim, his wife, and his son. Jim insisted that I would love it "back East." He told me that I needed to see the farming lifestyle his sister and her family lived. Since I trusted him, I heeded his advice when I bought the ticket in February of 2013. The trip wasn't until June.

Prior to setting off on the first Ohio adventure, I had been content living in Northern Nevada. I had a serious boyfriend, Jack, who I had been infatuated with for over six years. We lived together for most of that time, and although we loved each other deeply and existed well enough together, we came to a point where we realized we should go our separate ways. My world seemingly came crashing down after our breakup on Memorial weekend of that year. I was utterly thankful to have this getaway already planned with people I loved and trusted and who cared deeply for me. For those who understand the stupor that can occur after such heartbreak, you can imagine how I had one foot in reality and one foot out of reality as I traveled to an unfamiliar part of the country. And for those of you fortunate enough to not know this haze I am referring to, it might be comforting in the future to know it is part of the process of moving forward. Hopefully, you will have supportive friends and family around to help you get through it and perhaps some sort of adventure or distraction awaiting you while you heal. Life has a way of providing recovery, growth, and excitement at just the right time. For me, this rang true during my adventure to Ohio.

The beginning of this journey is somewhat hard for me to recount. It seems so long ago that the farm in Ohio was ever foreign to me, and the way my heart ached at the time still makes it difficult for me pull everything to the forefront of my mind. Luckily, I relied heavily on my journal at the time, eager to take down every detail, to immerse myself in my writing, and to focus on something other than rebuilding a new life without Jack.

Ohio Adventure Journal Entries

June 22, 2013

The lovely James and Beatrice Reed live on approximately 186 acres of farmland near the town of Hepburn, Ohio, which is not too far from the capital city, Columbus. On this specific trip, we will be celebrating James Senior's eighty-ninth birthday. They call him Pop. Bee, short for Beatrice, is eighty-four. They are both extremely sharp, pleasant, and welcoming. I am so grateful to be staying in their home.

Their farm was built in the 1830s and has since had many additions and renovations done to it. The impressive wood beams exposed throughout the house express the craftsmanship of the architecture. This decadent two-story home has six bedrooms, three bathrooms, a den, a study, a living room, a dining room, a kitchen, a solar room, and what seem to be endless hallways. There are four barns, a silo, and many beautiful gardens on the property. Some gardens are filled with many varieties of flowers, and one huge enclosed garden is abundant with rows of delicious herbs and vegetables, such as garlic, peas, squash, tomatoes, and onions.

Both James and Bee are from New Jersey, and they met through mutual friends in their early twenties. They have been married sixty-two years. They moved around a bit following James's career and eventually landed in Ohio where they raised their children. They moved to their current residence forty-one years ago.

Together, James and Bee have six children, five of whom are still alive. They tragically lost one daughter, Laura, to cancer at a very young age. In order of birth, there is Jim, Cindy, Ellen, Deborah, Laura, and Greg.

James Senior was a professor at Ohio State University, and Bee, after raising their children, went back to school to get her master's degree and worked as a social worker until retirement. She founded an organization called Change For The Family, and it advocated and supported the tragic issues of domestic violence. To this day, Bee is still involved in her foundation.

Bee, more than anything, loves to garden. She loves animals and her family too, but it's no secret that her soul thrives when she is maintaining her passion while getting her hands dirty in her many garden beds. The vast array of gardens each carry a name: the Rock Garden, the Wall Garden, the Pond Garden, the North Garden, the Vegetable Garden, and so on.

In her younger years, she had horses, and she spent most of her life riding them and teaching her children and grandchildren to ride. Their property has an excellent set up for horses, with a gorgeous four-stall barn, a few fenced pastures, and acres of woods and trails to ride. It's been years since they owned a horse; however, they still host a hunt program every so often on their trails.

The hunt is short for fox hunting, which is a sport performed on horseback. It is traditionally done with hound dogs and a group of trained huntsman. The hounds are released to track a fox, and they are followed by the people on horses. The sport requires a certain attire and etiquette that attract a particular crowd. It is a pastime enjoyed by somewhat more affluent participants. The Reeds have hosted the hunt on their property for years.

As I've met and learned more about each of the family members, I have observed how similar in heart they all are, yet they vary quite greatly in demeanor and spirit. Each of them is quite generous and loving in their own lives and passions. It's clear a strong sense of family values binds this bunch.

Jim, short for James Junior, I've learned, is the oldest brother. The more I see him around his family, the more I've come to realize he's servant-hearted in regards to his family. Even though he, his wife, and their son live some 2,000 miles away, I can tell how close he is to them.

Cindy, who is one year and one day younger than Jim, is free-spirited and adventurous. At seventeen years old, she moved to Mexico City to study at the university. She stayed in South America for a few years and had her first child, Leah, there. After the sudden loss of Leah's father, Cindy moved back to Ohio where she eventually remarried a cattle farmer named Bruce. They live about an hour from her parents' farm. Leah lives in New York City with her husband and young son. Cindy also has two other grown children, Annie and Thomas, who live on their own farms on adjacent properties to their parents', and they also work as cattle and grain farmers with their father, Bruce. Cindy is intuitive and a spreader of peace and joy. She works as a yoga instructor and loves to play music.

The next eldest child is Ellen, who is sweet, upbeat, and has a knack for organization. She lives in Asheville, North Carolina, with her husband, Tim, and their teenage son, Seth. She seems to be a very structured woman who loves her dogs and shopping. She is compassionate, fit, and fun-loving. She and Cindy seem to have a close and lively friendship.

Then comes Deborah, who carries a heart of gold filled with energy and enthusiasm. She lives about forty-five minutes from her folks, James and Bee, with her husband, Mack, and their teenage children, Mary and Jacob. They have a small farm on their property, and Deborah also works both as a teacher and at a local grocery store. Deborah is a giver. She is extremely loving and family oriented. She seems to be thoughtful and dependable.

The youngest son's name is Greg. I met him once in Reno years ago. He is due to arrive with his family the day we depart, so I might not get to meet them. What I know of Greg is that he lives in Tennessee, works with computers, and has graciously adopted his two daughters whom he calls his own.

As today nears its end, only three short days since my arrival, I am starting to feel a sense of peace with where I am. I am exactly where I ought to be, in the heart of the unknown, surrounded by warmth and genuine togetherness. I can't wait to see what else is in store!

June 23, 2013

This morning, in hopes to feed some endorphins into my body, I went for a run on a popular trail near Kenton, a small town about three miles as the crow flies from the farm. The trail stretches over twenty-five miles and connects the towns of Northwood and Dunkirk. It passes through the countryside as well as directly through the small, historic town of Kenton, Ohio. The trail is mostly covered by a tall tree canopy; however, there are sparing views of lush rolling hills and huge fields lined with long rows of grain. Occasionally, I'd pass by a dairy farm, and let me say, I could smell it long before it appeared in my sight. I saw many bicyclists and a few other runners today, and almost every person offered up a warm greeting or a friendly wave as I passed. I could get used to the benevolent attitudes, the unassuming friendliness here in Ohio.

Later in the morning, we went to the local farmer's market and enjoyed shopping for fresh produce and handmade crafts. I loved the sense of community I observed while meandering about the different booths. It was there I met a man who made art out of scrap metal and sold it at his retail booth. Coincidentally, he has an uncle who lives in Sparks, Nevada, which is just a stone's throw from my home in Reno. This man informed me that his uncle works at the Great Basin Brewery, last name Snider. I'll have to pop in and share the story with him sometime.

This afternoon, we'll be going down to Cindy's farm—well, actually, to her daughter Annie's property—to swim in her pool and have dinner. It's a nice hot summer day in June, so the pool will be refreshing. Thanks to Jim's influence, I will be venturing on to stay at Cindy's tonight and hopefully on to Annie's from there. I don't want to be intruding on anyone, but I know there is more I crave to see and do! In any case, I am enjoying it here at Bee's very much, and I'm sure I'll be able to find some way to earn my keep wherever I land. I certainly look forward to meeting new people and learning from them as well as sharing new experiences. Boy, am I lucky to be here and feel so welcomed!

Yesterday afternoon, Cindy, Bee, Mary, and I went mushroom hunting! That was my first experience searching the woods for mushrooms. Although we had no luck, it was wonderful to hear how much Cindy knows about the plants, trees, and various mushrooms that grow in this region. Cindy is involved in a mushroom foray where she searches for and identifies various mushrooms in the Central Ohio Valley. The nature here varies greatly from the High Sierra Desert back home. The Midwest woods are invigorating and full of life, with vast array of flora and fauna. The vibrant green and brown hues cover the surroundings in a natural camouflage—my favorite!

My soul feels genuinely connected with the earth here. I have thoroughly enjoyed my time exploring the farm. I ventured up a few hunters' tree stands throughout the property, letting my curiosity lead the way. It blows my mind that I have never experienced anything like this before! I felt like John Muir as I explored different perspectives of the unfamiliar land. Who knew I would find the Ohio country so inspiring and intoxicating?

The scenery is frequently picturesque, and the people are so kind—well, at least the ones I have been fortunate enough to meet thus far. I must comment on how well-spoken and well-mannered this particular family seems to be, probably due to the fact that Pop was a professor. I have heard there are rednecks and hillbillies not too far from here though :-). I hope to meet some of them folks too! Nonetheless, being around the Reed family sure does incline me to think a little more before I speak. Around them, I'm more aware of how often I utter words such as "whatever," "stuff," and "like" in a sentence. Each family member seems to be quite forgiving of my less-than-proper vernacular though.
Now it's time to pack my things so I may mosey on to the next farm experience!

June 24, 2013
As I sit anxiously pondering the events that may or may not unfold today, I can't help but feel warmth creep over my soul as I hear the birds chirping in the distance,

greeting each other with their morning "hellos" and "cheerios." I'm sitting alone on a sill in one of Annie's guest bedrooms. The mild hum of the pool's aerator is one of the many sounds I can hear around me. I don't normally wake with the sun, but the excitement of the unknown reminded me that I don't want to miss a thing! Oh! I just heard a door close. I must be on my way…

(Later that day.) Sorry about that! Let me fill you in on what happened today. We started the day at what Annie calls "headquarters," which is Bruce and Cindy's house. It sits tucked back on a half mile lane among slightly undulating fields and woods, accompanied by some fifteen horses in a glorious and unique two-story barn. We went for a nice, long, and productive horseback ride. As well as bonding and getting to know each other, Annie and I checked on a few different groups of cattle to make sure all of the pregnant heifers were doing okay. Annie would carefully inspect the newest calves to make sure they looked healthy. It took a few hours to ride through the countryside and complete our tasks. I literally felt like I was living in a dream!

The weather was perfect, and during our ride, Annie and I made a deep connection. She is simply delightful—I'd bet anyone who knows her would agree. She is down-to-earth, happy, and has a great sense of humor. She is intelligent and hardworking. It's hard to believe she is a farmer because, along with incredible personality attributes, she has a similar resemblance and build to a mix between Natalie Portman and Cindy Crawford. No joke! She's drop dead gorgeous. Her brother Thomas seems to be cut from the same cloth, and he too is hardworking and kind-hearted. However, his demeanor is a little more serious. But I have noticed that he does not walk by an animal without giving it a welcoming and warm pet. It's so refreshing to be around this family.

On my ride with Annie, I met one of their neighbors, Mr. Park, who is ninety-one years old. He was out cheerfully tending his beautifully symmetrical garden, which appeared to be blooming to his pleasure. We stayed on the horses and exchanged some neighborly words. He seemed like a jolly fellow and was very proud of his plants.

On horseback, we then stopped under a mulberry tree and ate a few freshly picked berries for a snack. I've never picked berries off a branch with my butt in a saddle. It was just like a scene from one of those old timey movies.

After we finished our ride and took the horses back to the barn, we then headed in Annie's truck to a nearby, small town named Cairo to run a few errands. This town's main street has only one stop sign. We went to the small feed mill to get some mineral for the cattle and the guys working there obviously knew Annie quite well.

"Well, howdy, fellas!" Annie exclaimed.

"Hey, Annie! How you doin' today?"

"Oh, I'm just finer than a frog's hair! This is my friend Karissa. She's visiting us from out west. She thinks she wants to be a farmer."

They all laughed as I gave a shy hello.

"Well, you're learning from Lima's finest," one guy said.

"We just need mineral today. I forgot to get it yesterday, and ol' Bruce isn't too pleased with me," she candidly explained.

"Sure thing. Just pull around back, and we'll take care of it."

"Thanks! Just put it on the account, will ya?" she gestured her hand to signal our departure as she swiftly turned and led us back to the truck.

The guys loaded our order into her white, single cab Ford pickup truck.

It wasn't long until we were headed back to the feedlot to continue the day's work. We started by greasing the rake the family uses for their hay. This rake is not like something you use to gather leaves in the yard. This piece of equipment is larger than two Ford Tauruses lined up bumper to bumper and resembles a praying mantis dressed as a porcupine. It is meant to be pulled behind a tractor over freshly mowed field hay in order to rake it into piles that can then be baled and stored for later use. Annie also had me help move some equipment around the property. Oh, how I love being useful! But, eventually, we came to a point where there wasn't much else for me to do as far as farm work goes, so I headed to over to headquarters to grab some goodies for dinner.

Since I love to cook, I volunteered to make dinner that evening. At Cindy's house, aka headquarters, I was able to grab a few herbs and vegetables from her garden, and it turned out she had just what I needed to fix a lovely meal. Cindy's garden was immaculate. She was tending to her blueberry bushes when I pulled up and announced my mission. She let me peruse the rows of veggies that were ready to harvest. I grabbed cilantro and garlic as well as some fresh lettuce. When I was finished, she brought me some blueberries that she'd gathered, and she welcomed me to take anything from her fridge as well. With her permission, I grabbed a ripe mango and some tomatoes. Thanks to her, there was no need to go to the store.

I made my way back to Annie's house. I gave her a quick call to let her know what I was up to and also to get a few basic instructions from her. She told me about some pork chops that she had in the freezer and encouraged me to thaw them out for the meal that evening. She also informed me that she would be inviting a few friends over and her roommate would join us as well, so I ought to make enough food for the group. And what a group it turned out to be!

Annie's friends and roomie welcomed me with warm hearts and great interest as we prepared and shared a delicious meal together. We grilled the pork on the barbeque while drinking beers and swapping stories. These country boys and their wild sense of amusement made the mood light. At one point, one of the guys laid spread-eagle on the kitchen floor while sharing a story about who-knows-what, but the hoots and hollers left the lot of us teary-eyed from the laughter. I made some couscous from a box they had in the pantry. That dish provided a good half hour of entertainment as the guys hilariously mocked the name. We also prepped a fresh salad with Cindy's lettuce and tomatoes, and of course, I made a tasty sauce for meal. We ate and drank and talked into the late hours of the night.

I now sit here in bed, trying to recap this perfect day, knowing I have an early morning tomorrow, but not wanting to miss a precious detail of my experience. I am eager to see what more will come of this Ohio adventure!

I had only planned to stay with Annie for a couple days of my trip for a few reasons. First of all, I didn't know her very well, so I wasn't trying to overstay my welcome or be an inconvenience to her or her family. Secondly, farmers are busy, and there was only so much time in a day for Annie to be my tour guide and provide answers to all of the inquiries I had, even though she surpassed my expectations exponentially. I tried to utilize my brief stint to see all that I hoped to see as far as the life of a farmer goes, but I also intentionally gave myself the time to feel my feelings, reflect on my experiences, and authentically observe the course I was on, not only physically, but emotionally as well.

In addition to spending a couple days getting my farmer on with Annie, her mother Cindy enhanced my time by inviting me to participate in a few complimentary yoga classes at her studio. I was submerged in a restorative journey that gently caressed the uncontrollable ache that resided within me. The random occasions of remembering my broken heart competed with the truths of my reality at the time. I was in a place that was so unfamiliar to me, but I felt right at home. I knew I was exactly where I needed to be. I was so preoccupied with the stimulations and energy of my surroundings that I didn't realize the healing that was occurring as each moment passed.

Although the short venture to Lima filled me with wonderment, I was due to head back to the Reed farm for the annual celebration that brought us to Ohio in the first place: Pop's birthday. He was turning eighty-nine, and celebrating birthdays in preeminent fashion was a tradition for the clan. I couldn't wait to gather with all of the people I'd gotten to know during my vacation. I eagerly anticipated seeing Jim so I could share with him all that I had done in the past few days. I also wanted to thank him for insisting I join him on this endeavor; after all, it was his idea for me to come. The plan was for me to ride up to the party with Cindy after I spent one last day imitating the life of a farmer.

The day we were due to head to the grandparents' farm, there was a major problem in one of the fields near the feedlot. A mother heifer struggled to give birth to her calf. On the Reynolds' farm, it was more common for an animal to experience delivery alone than it was for a human to get involved in the process, as this can cause stress to both the mother and baby, but sometimes the farmers needed to step in and assist mother nature. This particular birth traumatically left the mother paralyzed in her hind legs. We eventually found out that a pinched nerve occurred because of the size of the newborn calf, but in the midst of it, all hands were called on deck. Annie and Bruce took the lead in delegating strategic tasks to keep the heifer and calf alive and safe.

The first call to order was to get the newborn to safety, which clearly pissed off the immobile momma. The calf was soaked in goop, having just left the womb, and without hesitation, Annie bent down to gently pick him up. She then carried him to the barn where she could keep him contained and try to get him to eat. During calving season, the farmers kept cow's milk on deck for situations such as this. Not knowing what else to do, I followed her and witnessed the care and concern she gave to this new little life. He was weak and innocent, completely unaware of the turmoil encircled around his birth.

Once the calf was carefully secured, Bruce brought over a tractor and giant sling in preparation for the next step. Later, they told me that the sling was a contraption they almost never had to use, but in this case, it was the only option, and they needed to act fast. The sling was a huge, tarp-like blanket designed to hold a quadruped of that size. It had chains attached to various ends, and those chains could be connected to the fork of the tractor that would hoist the animal and allow it to be hauled off of the open field. Annie, Bruce, Thomas, and I gathered at a safe distance around the 1,200-plus-pound, agonizing animal. We cautiously laid the sling on the ground beside the cow. Annie bravely dictated our moves as we roped the animal's head and each of the front and hind legs in order to roll her massive body onto the sling. Can you imagine moving an animal that size with only four people?

Once we had enough leverage from the different ropes, and on Annie's count, we pulled in sync with tremendous effort and rolled the faltering beast just enough to get her on the sling.

"Okay, Karissa, let go of the rope and stand back!" Annie yelled, probably because I had little experience with the potential danger that the situation brought.

I listened to her command and understood that my help was no longer needed. I made my way to check on the calf, also knowing to keep my distance from him as well. I gazed at him curled up on some straw and felt a connection to his innocence, wondering if he realized the perplexities of the situation. Once I was alone, I cried. I cried for the joy of birth that I just witnessed. I cried for the trauma the heifer endured and the affliction she suffered, and I empathized with the emotions she exhibited. The distraught look in her eyes expressed the panic and fear she must have been feeling. I cried because I felt like I encountered a powerful truth about relying on those around you for help when you just can't do it alone. It gave me a hope that in the midst of suffering, there will be relief.

Just a few minutes after the initial endorphin-pumping ordeal, the astounding image of a bright red tractor driving toward the covered farm building toting a dangling cow brought tears of joy to my ambivalent spirit. This vision made an impression on me that I'll likely never forget. I mean, how often do you see a cow hanging in midair?

There wasn't much else to do once the trio erected the hurt animal, sling and all, onto a beam in the barn. A veterinarian was already en route, and they informed me that the due process for this type of situation was to leave the cow hanging for a time in hopes that, with the help of some medication, the pinched nerve would relieve itself so she would be able to walk again. Not long after the dust settled, Annie encouraged me to take her truck and head back to her house to get my things packed for my departure that afternoon. She could tell I was overwhelmed and emotional. We all were to some degree, but I wasn't used to this kind of mind-boggling excitement. I was actually relieved for the permission to leave.

Cindy picked me up just a few hours later, and she expressed compassion for the emotions I felt from having participated in the event. Her soft voice and sincerity wrapped my nerves, comforting me like a swaddle around a newborn baby. On our drive, she inquired about my overall well-being and attentively listened and prodded for me to recap my experience with her family in Ohio. With her free spirit and amiable nature, she graciously shared some of her own stories from her life that were filled with both adventure and awe. I felt a powerful connection with her from the pit of my being, and my heart grew in admiration for this incredible family.

* * *

I fell in love with the Ohio country and the people I was blessed to become acquainted with on my rejuvenating trip. They seemed to enjoy my curiosity and willingness to get my hands dirty, and I appreciated the hospitality and opportunities to enlarge my world that they generously presented to me.

"You should visit in the fall" was a common utterance I heard during those ten days in the early summer of 2013. This just reassured my belief that I had to come back. I wanted to know so much more about the life of a farmer. I wanted to connect deeper with these people who intrigued and impressed me to my core. My eyes had been opened to a whole new world, and just the thought of returning had me yearning for more.

Ache

Like I mentioned before, in 2013, I experienced the greatest romantic heartbreak of my life. I may have caused it and brought it upon myself, but needless to say, I still felt the gut-wrenching, lasting burn of a breakup. I went through it, and thanks to my best friends, my family, and *The Lord of the Rings* trilogy I repetitively watched, I survived. Truthfully, there were actually many months where I believed I wouldn't. I deeply contemplated altering who I was just so I could be with him, not because I didn't want to be alone, but because I didn't know how to accept that you could love someone so much and still know it wasn't going to work out. Now, I see why it's so important to learn these lessons young. They teach you to cope, get over it, and move on with your life so you can discover where the real magic lies.

Don't get me wrong. I loved Jack and wanted my future with him. To this day, I still talk about him, care about him, and occasionally show off pictures of our youthful shenanigans. But do I spend hours wishing we were together and pondering the what-ifs and the what-could've-beens? No, most certainly not. I have moved on from the idea that there is one true love of our lives, and I've learned to pour the energy and love I thought I was giving to him inside myself instead. My dad has joked about my ex, saying, "I feel bad for Jack. He was the guy you learned how to be a girlfriend with." And I suppose there's some truth to that joke.

I met Jack when I was nineteen years old at our mutual friend's house. I still remember scanning him up and down with his long white socks almost touching his black pants that were torn into below-the-knee shorts. He had a metal chain attached to his wallet, a white wife beater tank top, gorgeous bold eyes, and a bald head. After assessing him once or twice, I'd decided instantly he was going to be mine.

My best friend Sandy told me I had horrible taste in guys, but I'd say the same of her. She was with me the first night I stayed with Jack—however, that wasn't how I intended for the evening to go.

One night, Sandy and I were at a party in Carson City, even though we both lived in Reno at the time. She and I came down to the party together, and apparently after many repeated attempts of separating my face from Jack's, the damn bitch took my truck and drove it back to her house… about forty minutes away. Once I realized the predicament I was in, my knight (in shiny armor?) came to the rescue and took me back to his place.

Fast forward through the years: I moved back to Carson for work, he and I eventually moved in together, we moved back to Reno, we got dogs together, we went through jobs together, we lost loved ones together, we grew in love together, and then, eventually, we grew apart.

The idea that we had grown apart fully hit me during a Memorial Day weekend spent camping at Frenchman's Lake with some friends and family. I remember looking at everyone around us, and the harsh reality of where Jack and I stood slapped me hard across the face. While everyone else had changed, evolved, we stood still. His sister, who was single when we first met, was now married and had just had her first baby. She had brought little Lilly up to the campsite where we were staying, and I can still remember gazing at Lilly longingly, wondering when it'd be my turn. Another couple, who were mutual friends of ours, was also with us that weekend, and they had just gotten married and were expecting their first child. It seemed the people around me were following the natural progression in their lives, but we were not.

Actually, I think we need to rewind a bit.

Jack was a musician. I suffered much ridicule, as I'm sure he did for having this dream. Apparently, since so many people dream of being a rock star, it becomes too outlandish or fairytale-like for anyone with this dream to become successful. The difference for him, though, was that Jack was an exceptionally talented drummer. I don't say this because he was my boyfriend; I say this because I had ears, loved music, and have witnessed enough live performances to know a good drummer when I hear one. Jack had a gift when it came to playing his drums. He was consumed by it. Day in and day out, I'd watch him spend hours playing music, working on his drums, following other musicians, and spending his time and money on this true love of his.

I envied this focused dream. I envied his drive and passion and his ability to remain steadfast over the years to this one, single idea. And he was extraordinary at it. I spent years searching myself for a dream. What did I love? What did I want to do? What was I exceptional at? I couldn't pinpoint anything. Although, I tried many things. I loved food and to travel, but many people shared those passions, and I wouldn't say I was a cut above in those areas, nor did they ignite that spark within me. Sure, I fancied myself a great cook, but I wasn't the next top chef. I also loved to write, but for years, I lacked the discipline or focus to actually come up with something other than a school paper for myself or a friend in need. To witness Jack's dream and his ability to achieve it only solidified in my mind my role as his girlfriend was to encourage him to stay focused. So, I did.

One night, after he abruptly lost his job, I found Jack sitting out in the backyard of our rental house. He was pretty down and quiet, and to be honest, I don't remember how exactly the conversation went, but I do remember I had only seen him this upset one previous time in our many years together. I'm told that, for men, having a job is an identifying role for their ego. As a woman, I don't understand this as much, but I can grasp it. I remember asking Jack that if there was anything in the world he could do, what would it be, and he replied, "Play music." I let him know that I would support him wholeheartedly and financially for him to pursue that dream.

Although at the time it seemed like the right thing to do, this, I believe, was the moment when I started to value Jack and his dreams over myself and my dreams, which is a dangerous and toxic recipe for a relationship. In a healthy relationship, I've learned, there needs to be a mutual balance of individuality, support, encouragement, and give and take. I don't want this to come off like Jack didn't support me in anything I did, because he did, and very much so. I was always busy and accomplished many goals, had many ideas, and traveled all over during our time together, and he loved me through all of it. The problem here lay in me. At some point, I began to place my value of who I was as an individual on being fully supportive of him. I put my own ambitions on the back burner. I may have even tossed them out with the bath water.

Now, this book isn't about the story of Karissa and Jack, so there are many years and many details not to be included here, but I'd like to give some more perspective on who I am. I am a control freak—well, at least I *was*. I have spent the past few years aiming to be less manipulative and conniving and just trying to go with the flow of things. But, oh, does the Lord know how much I want my way and how I will figure out a way to get it. I think I inherited this trait from my mother.

Anyway, I think it must have been 2010 or so when I decided I wanted to marry Jack. We'd been dating a few years, and we pretty much acted as if we were married. And since that was the road I wanted to go down, I figured I could make it happen. Hmm, how romantic, right? No. How narcissistic. Needless to say, the conversation came up with his mother and again with my mother, and before long, we all wanted us to get married…except, perhaps, one important person: the groom.

I have a very strong personality, and as I've said before, he truly did love me and supported me in my many endeavors; so, I feel like Jack went along with the whole thing as he'd figured he should. After all, we *were* a sharp couple. But let me tell you how this all really went down. My mother had given us some of her old rings, one being her engagement ring from my father. Now, when I say given to *us*, I mean given to *me*. "We" then had those rings melted down and redesigned into a one-of-a-kind engagement ring and wedding band. This whole process took about five months. I was elated and in control. The rings came out gorgeous, and I was obsessed. Then, I gave them to Jack like, "Here, honey. When you're ready, I'm ready!"

Ugh. Gross. Of course, I only now think that, but at the time, I had spent months wondering and hoping and anticipating when he would pop the question. I mean, c'mon, I put the ball on the T, placed the bat in his hands, showed him where to stand—the rest was simple! Again, how romantic. And, let me tell you, this was only one of the many, stupid, controlling things I did in our relationship. Sure, I did it with a smile on my face and perhaps the best of intentions, but let me say this loud and clear: IF HE'S NOT BUYING THE RING, THEN HE PROBABLY DOESN'T WANT TO GET MARRIED!

Despite all the red flags, I got my way, and he proposed. It was subtle and sweet, just like him. I couldn't wait to share the news and show off my ring. I glowed. I was a food server, so I made sure to show every one of the customers my unique engagement ring and allow the love I felt to be seen. Everything was seemingly perfect in my blinded eyes. I was an ecstatic twenty-three-year-old ready to settle down and start my life with the man I loved. I allowed the glory and excitement to radiate from me for some time.

Having a wedding and getting married to Jack had me on a unique high and was truly my main focus, just like many other brides-to-be who get caught up in the captivating ideals of matrimony. It was only a few short weeks after my engagement that I was stopped dead in my tracks by some devastating news. One of the closest friends I had ever had, Eric, was killed in a car accident. I was no longer high on the thought of marriage. I was heartbroken like I had never been before. I felt lost. I felt guilty. I felt helpless. I felt confused and tormented. I wanted to be there for his family. I wanted to have answers. I wanted to know why. *Why? Why did this happen? How could this happen? What the fuck?!*

In my early twenties, I sort of believed in God, so I was compelled to figure out how this was acceptable. If there was a God, then how could He allow such an amazing, love- and life-filled person to be taken from us? In the span of one month, life as I knew it changed greatly. How could one month of life completely encompass the entire spectrum of emotions? I no longer felt high. I was low, nearly the lowest I'd ever been.

This painful, life-altering news sent me on an answer-seeking journey. I let the ideas of date setting, cake tasting, and obsessive planning fade into oblivion as I found myself on a hot pursuit to find this so-called God and confront Him face-to-face to hear why the hell He would rip Eric from this world. I had experienced some loss before the loss of Eric, but his death uprooted me.

That year, I submerged myself in asking questions. I asked myself questions. I asked others questions. I talked to people, all sorts of people—old, young, divorced, widowed, Christians, atheists, hardworking, lazy, wealthy, healthy, sick, poor, veterans, and average Joes. I asked them about their experiences with death. I asked them how they had coped, or would cope, or should cope. I asked them what they thought, how they thought, and why they thought. I wanted to hear who believed what and why.

I visited churches and found myself joining Bible studies and retreats. I was relentlessly looking for answers in people. I observed and watched and asked and tried to connect. Although I befriended some interesting, compassionate people, I was searching for God. I was searching for help and answers and really any information that made this life make sense. For a time, my quest was fruitless. And in those months, I began to change—but not for the better.

In November of that same year, more devastation wreaked havoc in my world when my five-year-old little brother suffered a traumatic brain injury. He got kicked in the head by a horse and was care-flighted to the emergency room with a skull fracture. It did not look good for him. I remember my dad telling me that he saw his brains among the gore that oozed out of his head wound. My poor father.

That night, I was in another realm while we sat in a private hospital waiting room. We sat in the room as a family, but we were all in our own worlds for those dreadful hours, each of us clinging only to ourselves, for we had no comfort to give each other. I wish I could have consoled my family, but I was relentlessly praying to be delivered from the nightmare I was in.

I literally thank God my brother recovered from that incident as well as he did. It was a rough couple of years for my dad and stepmom, to say the least, but my little brother survived. The medical professionals harmonized that, "Kids bounce back better and faster than adults with these types of injuries."

That horrible incident was the final straw that sent me to dive even deeper into a journey of answer-seeking. Initially, I had tried to find comfort and support in the newly established relationships I had at the church. I attempted to cling to the "program" to receive healing and understanding of all that life presented to me that year. But I only felt more alone and disconnected. I was left with the grueling reality that all of these people, these "Christian people," were just that—people. And in that, they were not "my people." So, with their hearts consumed in their own lives and their opinions wrapped up in their own perspectives, they were not the answers to the questions I had. They were not comforting my tears or healing the wounds I felt within. The wedge between myself and the people around me began to grow deeper.

As the emotional angst grew within me, I isolated myself with each uncertainty that life presented. Who could I depend on to keep me stable? On what foundation could I feel secure? Where could I find the unwavering sense of control that I sought?

It was during this time of my emotional instability that Jack "forgot" our anniversary. By now, it might be quite obvious that I took this mistake as a devastating blow to the straw house I'd built, but it was a breaking point for me. So, in this state of exasperation, I kicked Jack out of the house for a few months, and then, somehow, I expected we would still get married after that. We stuck it out for another year or so, but it didn't take more than an honest, heartbreaking conversation for us to end our relationship and agree that we were heading in different directions. Although that conversation left me broken and lost in a way I had never felt before, I was convicted that there was more to life than what he and I were living, and I was determined to seek it, regardless of where that left him.

Little did I know, a healing, magical adventure was just around the corner.

Motion

In an attempt to distract myself from dwelling on what was or what could have been, I purposefully kept myself busy. I picked up a second serving job and submerged myself in activities that filled my calendar and my mind. I committed to different athletic events and races as a means to discipline myself in healthy training routines so I wouldn't fall back into old habits and self-destructive behaviors. Those pursuits didn't keep my head completely out of the water of woe, but they seemed to serve as floatation devices, for a while, nonetheless. Now at twenty-five years old, I felt a stirring within me, a call for action, if you will. The magic from my first Ohio adventure opened my eyes to the allure of the great unknown and the rewards that can be found in going new places and meeting new people. So, I opted to move forward. The moves I made were rather blind and incidental, but I made the efforts to forge ahead. For at least the immediate future, I aimed for changes that pulled me out of my comfort zone.

My heart would compel me to move, and I paid attention and listened to it like an explorer reads his compass. I started saying yes to favorable propositions that were presented to me. I went on a few random dates with prospects who tickled my fancy. I accepted an offer for a management position at the casino, even though that only panned out for a short time. And I even tested the waters as a bartender when a friend of mine said he needed an extra hand at the bar he managed. I began to adopt the mindset that I would just keep trying new things and see where the paths might lead. I rolled with the punches. And after enduring the first holiday season without being intertwined in all that comes with being in a committed relationship, I decided to set sail into the new year with a new mindset. I would intentionally seek adventures bigger than those of my past. I embraced the idea that doors behind me were closing, and I harnessed excitement for walking through new doors of opportunity that were opening in front of me. This took some courage and steadfastness and a connection within myself that dulled out the naysayers and dream crushers. I welcomed the realization that flowing against the grain is often met with discouragement and disdain from those who have contently enjoyed the current.

It seemed with each step I took, something magical was waiting just around the bend. Things were falling into place before my very eyes, although it was hindsight that allowed me to see it all more clearly. As I kept moving forward, I began to see how each circumstance played upon the next. I picked up extra work just to keep myself distracted, but all of the extra money I'd been earning made it easier for me to pursue more costly endeavors. I was fortunate to have people in my life that invited me to explore new territories, and now I had the means to do it. By this time, I had developed excellent money management skills. This practice allowed me to feel in somewhat control of my livelihood so when I wanted to take time off or spend my money, I could do it without too much stress. And luckily for me at the time, my waitress positions proved to be very flexible as far as scheduling and requesting time off. This gave me a sense of freedom that I quickly learned I valued greatly in my life. And as it turned out, my priorities shifted and fell into place because of this freedom.

For my first wide-eyed endeavor, in February of 2014, I spent two weeks in San Miguel de Allende, Mexico, with the mother of my dear friend Eric, who we tragically lost just a few years prior, and whom, ultimately, I have to thank for setting my world on fire and changing my path. She'd found solace in the beautiful city tucked in the mountains south of the border. We shared a deep bond, so when she extended the invitation to join her, I didn't hesitate to accept. Those weeks in Mexico were peaceful and quiet. I felt myself healing, the unfamiliar territory and the different cultures sewing up old wounds with the sheer magic of their newness. Time seemed to move slower, and our days were filled with long walks, long naps, and long meals.

I spent hours during that trip introspectively delving into parts of my mind that had been foggy and dormant for some time. I read the book *The Shack* by William Paul Young, and I journaled about my thoughts, feelings, and reflections on the pains I'd been harboring at the time. It gave me confidence to keep moving and the strength to attempt to let go of the past.

I returned from Mexico with hardly a tan, but instead with a stain of reality and vision in my heart. I had intimately experienced time and conversation with a joyful woman who possessed the determination to persevere and find beauty and peace in her darkened world. She exposed me to cultural history and palette-expanding concoctions, but far more impactful was her compassionate friendship and the exuberant wisdom she revealed to me on that trip. For the first time in a long time, I felt full, having feasted on a world so different from mine, and I was reminded that it is through the relationships we foster that we can feel connected, alive, and somewhat okay during seasons of brokenness.

Later that year, during the summer, my friend Charlotte, who I'd known since high school, experienced her own trying heartbreak. In an effort to conjure up an exciting distraction, we decided to take an impromptu road trip along the Pacific Coast Highway. We played the roles of two best friends crammed in a car beautifully. On our adventure, we followed our favorite hip-hop group from San Diego to Chico, California. We ventured at our own pace and really had no place to be at any specific time, other than the concerts that were spread a few days apart, but even so, we were only partially committed to attending the shows as they served to be more like guides points for our vacation. We spent a weekend strolling the streets of San Francisco. We endured a marathon-like day at Disneyland. And we made pit stops at diners, cliffsides, and serene oceanside spots that called to our hearts along the way. We snapped photos of the good times and made room for rest and tear-filled conversations when we needed a break.

Like my trip to Mexico, this road trip bandaged parts of me I didn't even realize were wounded, but it also helped to sever the intricate ligaments that kept me tied to the life I was living. This gentle separation fueled my curious spirit, pushing me to continue on toward the ultimate transformation I would come to experience down the road. It showed me it was okay to change, and that I, in fact, needed change. It magnified my feelings of being a big fish in a small pond, and it generated in me a deep yearning for adventure, something my regular life could no longer fulfill.

This change in perspective on these trips contributed to my confidence and courage to see just what this big world had to offer, both near and far. It reminded me that when times are unsettling, you must take action and aim at something. It could be a getaway, it could be a distraction, or hell, it could be a blindfolded series of hollering "Yes please!" to the world, but ultimately, it is a motion of faith that makes what could be better than what is. And trust me, nothing grandiose can happen without meeting life with an open attitude, a thirsty spirit, or gesture that says, "I'm ready." And by this time, I. Was. Ready.

The next step in my unplanned plans was a trip back to Ohio to see what all the fuss was about during the fall season. I'd been planning this specific trip pretty much from the moment I left the first time. I looked forward to the long-waited reunion with the people and country I'd fallen in love with some year and a half before. I had stayed in touch with Annie, and we were both extremely excited to reconnect; after all, we were soul sisters at first sight. And this time around, I wouldn't be in the languor of heartbreak. I met my vacation with vigor and anticipation to learn, to grow, and to broaden my horizons.

When I landed at the airport in Columbus it, was the 8th of October. I was filled with energy, and I relished every ounce of excitement I felt for the days ahead of me. I made my way to the Enterprise car rental counter and was met with pleasure when the friendly gentleman at the counter informed me that he had upgraded my economy reservation to a midsize SUV without additional charges. I was rolling in style in a brand-new black Jeep Liberty, equipped with a Bluetooth radio and GPS navigation for my traveling pleasure. This surprise gave me an extra boost as it reminded me to appreciate the hidden joys that may be in store for me. I took my time driving to the farm, inadvertently getting lost on my way there, but I enjoyed the detours and backroads that advertised a part of the country I had yet to traverse.

In preparation for my return, Annie had planned activities, parties, and excursions for me to participate in for my basically the entirety of my visit. Some things she would join me in, but others, she sent me off for solo missions. That girl sure knew what would suit my fancy. She also knew which fun-loving, warm-welcoming people would enhance my experiences. I had no idea what was in store for me, but I was blessed to have a thoughtful and kickass event planner who would help me make the most out of this adventure. The perfected details of Annie's considerate ideas would eventually seal the deal for me to dream of making Ohio my home.

For this trip, I stayed at Annie's house the entire time. Her house was nicknamed "Sinner's Palace." This self-fulfilling prophecy of a title was deemed appropriate when Olivia, Annie's roommate, needed to put up some of her cousins while they were in town for a family wedding. Due to religious beliefs, Olivia's mother wouldn't allow unmarried couples to stay under her roof. Instead, her mother candidly announced they could stay down the road at "Sinner's Palace" if they insisted on bunking with their unbetrothed partners. Although this was a small comment made in jest, it wasn't long before they welcomed the name with amusement and proud proclamation. It was, however, kind of an oxymoron for anyone who knew the place because Annie was a do-gooder, a class valedictorian filled with integrity and manners, and Olivia's pleasant demeanor and polite poise was far from that of a hellion. The two, in fact, were more likely to raise animals and kindness rather than havoc and sin, but when a name sticks, it sticks. And I was quickly deemed a perfect addition to Sinner's Palace, or later simply known as SP. I was this random girl from Nevada, and everyone knows Nevadans only come from Las Vegas and we're all sinners who sling guns, shoot whiskey, and play the harlot while strolling the dirt roads in the Wild, Wild West, right? Needless to say, the SP title served as a long running joke for quite some time.

It didn't take me long to settle in at SP, and within forty-eight hours of being in Ohio, the gang took me out to my first ever county fair. The highlight of the evening was to be the combine derby, an event where combines, which are large farming machines that are used to harvest grains, are souped-up and decked out to smash each other derby-style in a large dirt pit surrounded by grandstands filled with beer-drinking onlookers. I love monster trucks and have always been quite fond of mudslinging derbies, so I eagerly anticipated this event.

When we arrived at the fair, we met up with some of Annie's friends and mingled while we munched on fair food that I'd never tried, including fried oysters and Ohio-famous buckeyes, which were balls of peanut butter dipped in chocolate. These delicacies were named after the prevalent Ohio state tree that bared the nuts these tasty treats resembled.

After our appetites were satiated, we moseyed through the various fair tents that were filled with handmade crafts, homegrown goods, and artistically displayed entries. There were award winning edibles like delicious pies, blemish-free vegetables, and perfected preserves. We posed for pictures with massive pumpkins and charming scare-crows, and then Annie announced that the best was yet to come. We crossed the dimly lit fairgrounds, making our way from the crowded carnival side that housed the food and activities and meandered toward the livestock area.

Massive barns made temporary holding pens for locally-raised, prize-winning animals like hogs, lambs, steers, and horses. We spent our time casually looking at the animals, and we'd stop and spend time with different breeds, petting them when we were allowed. Annie shared her knowledge with me about what qualifies certain animals to participate and how the community worked together to support the fair. To my amazement, the Budweiser Clydesdales were invited to the Allen County Fair that year, and we were able to see these massive creatures up close. We weren't allowed to touch them, but just standing beside the enormous horses filled me with satisfaction and glee. Moment by moment, my fondness grew for this country life that was so unfamiliar to me. I radiated with high hopes for what more was to come.

Since I was so eager to learn all about cattle farming, I spent as much time as I could with Annie at work while trying not to be in the way, which she reassured was far from the case. As it turned out, they enjoyed having an extra pair of working hands on the farm just as much as I enjoyed doing dirty jobs. Annie started me on a task where I was knee-deep in cow dung, also referred to as bedding the stalls. She equipped me with muck boots and a pitchfork as I got down and dirty with the cows at the feedlot—and I loved every stinking minute of it.

She took me to help her mend fences and repair machinery, all the while explaining to me the functions, necessities, and processes of each task. I learned the balance of a farmer's life relies upon many factors. Sure, they must put in the long days of hard work, but being a farmer requires far more than just physical ability and strength; it also demands a great deal of knowledge, communication, prioritization, diligence, and the anticipation of frequent disruptions. When the well-being of animals and crops are at stake, there is a delicate dance between what ought to be done and what needs to be done. And this family had mastered that dance.

I loved hearing the phrase, "You've got to make hay with the sun's out." It reminded me to keep my focus, to consider the appropriate times for addressing each task. This was definitely a farmer's saying, but I thought it pertained to life as well. When opportunities are at hand, it's important to pour energy into a specific focus when the time, place, and weather permit. For me, I was in a place where I wanted to gain a better understanding of just what it meant to be a farmer. But there was something else stirring within me, a pining to explore a greater unknown.

The next few days, I continued to help around the farm in the small ways that I could, but I also wanted to see what else the Midwest had to offer through my own speculative lens.

The farm was tucked at the very edge of where the foothills of the Appalachian Mountains met the vast plains of the Midwest. To the east, the land began to undulate, and to the west, the open sky filled the horizon. Annie told me about a popular place called Hocking Hills, which was home to natural waterfalls and serene wilderness. She encouraged me to take the drive to go explore. I didn't hesitate to heed her advice and set out for a day of solitude in yet another new setting.

It was true: Ohio in the fall surely was a sight to see. The aging leaves of the trees displayed an array of autumn tones in pleasant, eye-catching harmonies. The seemingly endless fields were overgrown with plenty of tremendous cornstalks that too had turned from the vibrant green I'd seen in the previous summer to a pale yellow in preparation to donate their yield. At that time of year, the countryside stirred as farmers steadily worked to reap their hard-earned harvest, and oversized tractors caused delays on the two-lane roads quite frequently. I felt like I was in another world when I passed by a few Amish homesteads that were visually different from their gas-guzzling neighbors. One farm even had a horse-drawn plow working the grounds.

There was no cell phone service in the Hocking Hills, which made my experience that much better since I couldn't be distracted by worlds that were far away, a gentle encouragement to be in the present moment. I strolled the paths that led to caves and crags with delight. At this time, there was only a little bit of water glistening among the formations, but I was told during the spring the waterfalls would roar. I made friendly gestures to passersby and didn't hesitate to offer my assistance to couples and families when there was a photo op. Each of them graciously extended to return the favor. I soaked in the aroma of dew from the forest around me and basked in the ambiance of this mini getaway. Being in nature has always revitalized my soul; pairing this truth with my absorbent mindset confirmed for me that I was in the right place at the right time. I was searching for contentment within, and that is exactly what I found.

When I returned from my escapade, I was in for a real treat! Sinner's Palace was throwing their annual pumpkin carving party that weekend, and the girls were gathered around the kitchen table making plans for the ghoulish decorations and festive recipes. With the help of Pinterest, they planned dishes like graveyard bean dip, Jack-O-Lantern guacamole, and Olivia's famous sangria for the cauldron. I loved the thoughtfulness and attention to detail this gang gave when throwing a party. Annie set up large tables in rows in her detached garage so the partygoers could all carve their pumpkins together. The food and drinks were to be scattered throughout, and the night would be capped with a bonfire in the pasture behind the garage. I was pumped!

Annie invited many friends to the party, and to my surprise, she informed her buddy Sean that I was eager to learn to hunt. He brought his compound bow and a large foam target to her house and set it up in the lawn out front. Before the sun went down, he spent some time teaching me how to shoot the bow, and he told me that if I felt comfortable, he'd take me out around the property to look for deer the next day. Things just kept getting better! And thanks to Annie, the opportunities to pursue my desires just kept rolling in.

Unfortunately, the bonfire and whiskey roused my spirits until the wee hours of the night. I slept soundly through half of the next day, and when I woke up, there was almost no trace of the party the night before. I felt a little guilty not contributing to the cleanup crew. As I staggered upstairs to get myself some coffee, I was the butt of many jokes due to the hour of the afternoon it was. Apparently, everyone else had been up for hours; Annie had already been to work and back. But I was elated to find Sean still there offering to take me hunting in the woods. He informed me that the early morning hours or just before the sun sets in the evening were the best times to go, so we still had the chance to quench my bloodlust.

Sean said that he was an advocate for teaching others to hunt, so he was just as excited as I was for the endeavor. He spoke with Thomas, Annie's brother, about where to go on the property and got permission to use some tree stands that belonged to other hunters that were already erected in the woods. Before we left, he informed me of some hunting insights to be prepared for: no scents, no talking, and don't shoot unless you know it's a kill shot. Sean brought his own shimmying stand so he could post up near me. We walked for about twenty minutes into the thick of the tall trees. Nervousness and excitement turned my stomach into its own little amusement park.

Birds whistled through the trees, woodpeckers hammering the tree trunks, and I waited in anticipation, jerking with excitement at each sound of crunching leaves or the whispering wind. I didn't speak a word as I sat some twenty feet in the air on two rickety pieces of metal, one just large enough to house my butt and the other for my feet. Sean supervised by pointing, smiling, and gesturing me to observe the trails where the potential white-tails might cross. To my dismay, nothing happened. By the time the sun went completely down and darkness began to fall, he called it a day.

Although our mission was a bust, to me it was enthralling and satisfying. I had successfully shot the bow and arrow at the target with enough competence that he'd taken me out for the real thing. To me, that was a little win. I relished in the experience that I was doing something I'd never done but wanted to do, and all in all, I was moving toward growth. I was embracing the unknown in hopes to make it known. I was taking steps to learn what I wanted to learn and to experience the unfamiliar calls of my heart. And if it weren't for me boldly sharing my ideas with Annie, and her scheming to help make my dreams come true, I wouldn't have had the experience of my first hunt.

In the time leading up to this two-week endeavor, I'd shed my old skin. I was no prisoner to the limiting beliefs that discouraged action and the constraining discomfort from the aches of my heart. I began to gently feed my curious spirit with the hope of tiny treasures I knew life had waiting for me. I embraced the hardships I'd faced in my life and allowed them to play their roles in my story, but I also learned to not let them define me. This growth did not come easy and certainly didn't happen overnight. It took time and patience, fortitude and effort. But by the time my vacation came to its end, I recognized the person in the mirror, but I also saw her in a whole new light. She was stronger, wiser, and braver. And upon seeing the image of a newer version of myself, I began to dream bigger. I began to ask myself, "What more could I be?"

Action

"If you want to really understand farming, you have to live it."

Annie smacked me with this truth after my second visit to Ohio when she invited me to come back for an entire season. It didn't take long for me to begin dreaming about how moving across the country to live on a farm could actually work. I imagined her basement would become my living quarters; I could fix it up as needed, clear out enough of the bugs and dirt to make it livable. I pictured learning from the farmers and picking up some part-time work as necessary to cover any extra financial needs I might incur. The more I fantasized about it, the more I realized I was really going to do this. I *could* really do this. And the notion that in order to live your desired reality, you must first believe your dreams could come true began to fully sink in.

When I decided that I would actually quit my job, leave my newly renovated house, pack my two dogs and any necessary belongings in my truck, and move across the country, the date was November 1, 2014. The decision to move came only a few short weeks after I'd returned from my second visit to Ohio, where all of the fantasies of me actually living on a farm were born. It's easy to dream of living where you spend a vacation, and it's probably a very common concept to dream about, so I didn't get too carried away at first. But after being home for just a short time, I knew it was really going to happen. You see, at this point, I had rekindled a "friendship" with Jack (you know, the "greatest romantic heartbreak I ever experienced"), and it had been many months of spending time with him and developing feelings again that allowed my imagination to run wild with what we could be this time around.

I had stayed in regular contact with Jack during my second stay in Ohio, sending pictures and recounting my experiences over the phone. It was marvelous and so comfortable. Not long after returning home to Nevada, I asked him via text message if he wanted to get back together. I mean, after all, we were acting as if we were, but we just hadn't had the conversation. But when he replied that he would hate to lose me to someone else, but he didn't want to ruin our friendship, I just knew. I knew it had to be over for good with him. I couldn't stand reliving the pain I had felt the previous year, and I also knew that our goals would never be in line. It took me a couple days of honest reflection to come to this point, but I do remember by the time the 1st of November rolled around, I had made the decision. It was time not only to move, but it was time to move on.

* * *

"Traveling East will bring you great reward."

I framed a fortune from a fortune cookie with those words and placed it in a conspicuous place in my room. I read that little piece of paper every single day. It is true about chasing your dreams—you must pursue them daily. So, I knew it was time to start gearing up to pursue this dream of traveling East to live on a cattle farm!

I began to write my goals and dreams out. I gave timelines and deadlines for all of the affairs I needed to get in order to make this dream a reality. I needed to save money. I needed to give my job notice that I would be leaving. I would need health insurance. What would I take with me to Ohio? What would I leave behind? What would I do with the stuff I left behind? How do I make this happen? I made lots of lists and had conversations with many friends, acquaintances, and bartenders in order to get as much input, perspective, and advice as possible.

I also knew I needed to speak with my family and loved ones to let them know my plans. I needed to figure out the details of leaving my brother behind and in charge of the house we'd purchased together. Would I still pay my half of the mortgage? Would I rent my room out? What about the unfinished ideas we wanted to pursue with home renovations? But most importantly, I needed to talk to Annie. I had to know if she was serious about inviting me to live with her and learn from her.

"Hey, Annie!" I said through the mouthpiece of my phone. "Are you sure I can live in your basement?" I asked.

"Hey, girl, hey!" she spoke with a positive and joyous tone as she welcomed the conversation with love and excitement. "As long as I have a place for my vet stuff, you are more than welcome to come live in my basement." She laughed as her tone implied that living in her basement would not be any sort of alluring luxury.

"Are you sure? I mean, I would have to bring my dogs… But I would totally fix it up to make it livable, and I wouldn't expect anything from you, except you know, to let me make some improvements and stuff," I humbly asserted.

"Well, I had this guy live down there for a few months, and he had some cats, and the cats had fleas, and I don't go down there hardly ever, so it's not like its clean… I mean, I got rid of all the fleas, but you've seen it. It's a mess!"

As she rambled off these random truths, my mind only heard positive reinforcement that she was saying yes. *This is it. It's going to happen!* I could barely contain my excitement.

Before we hung up, she reassured me she would do anything she could to help me with the transition and was looking forward to teaching me anything I would want to learn on the farm—all for the small price of cooking a few meals on the farm, she teased. Her kindness solidified that this was the right decision; Ohio was where I needed to be.

From that point on, I kicked my butt into high gear, crossing off items on my countless lists with eagerness and delight. I knew I needed this change. I knew it was the right thing to do. But what I didn't know was that taking this leap to go on this journey would completely affect the course of my future.

* * *

As with all respectable goals, you need a deadline, a time-bound goal that adds pressure to the situation. After confirming the move with Annie, I pulled out a calendar and picked a date: February 23, 2015. It was a Monday. Mondays are good days to start new things.

I knew that I wanted to be in Ohio before my twenty-seventh birthday. In choosing my departure date, I calculated that I would arrive in Ohio with enough time to settle in before celebrating the turning of my next year of life. I looked forward to spending my birthday with a wonderful family at a picturesque farm in a map-dot spot in the world. I had experienced firsthand how this family celebrated each other, and I couldn't wait to be the center of one of their highly enjoyable occasions. It was set. I would leave Reno in just over three months. Shit. Just. Got. Real.

I decided to only share my decision with a few people at first. Anyone who knows me knows that I *always* have a *million* ideas. My dad used to tell me that when I was little, I would excitedly announce, "Daddy, I have an idea!"

His response would be, "Great, kid. Now wait five minutes, and tell me both."

So, I knew to others this very much could have seemed to be just another idea I had that would eventually fade away in time, but I knew I was going to follow through with this one. For months, I kept my mouth shut, except for when I'd make the occasional joke that I wanted to go live on a farm in Ohio. A few of the people I did tell doubted me, so that only fueled my desire to prove them wrong. I felt a fire in my heart. I knew I was about to make a huge change.

There were some challenges and hurdles to overcome, but I'd say the biggest predicament, if you would call it that, was that my brother and I were in the middle of a huge kitchen remodel—and that kitchen remodel was my idea. (Hmm, weird.) We'd started the project in the summer of that year, and as with any home renovation, it took months longer than projected. So by late November, or early December of 2014, we still hadn't finished. Luckily though, by Christmastime, we were finally able to cook in the kitchen, which meant no longer having to only use plug-in appliances and do all of our dishes in the tiny bathroom sink. And by late January of 2015, we finally got our final inspection.

I still find the timing of my decision to move quite comical because I had spent months and thousands of dollars designing and working on building our new kitchen. Yes, my brother and I worked as a team, but being a woman and being the stubborn, bullheaded breed that I am, I was particular about many details of this project. This was my dream kitchen! We didn't just update cabinets and fixtures. We knocked out walls, moved windows and doors, added gas lines, and completely reoriented our entire first floor. We got all new appliances, beautiful marble countertops, tile floors, and dark Cherry wood cabinets. I just wanted it to look better, to be more functional, and to increase the value of our house.

Needless to say, this was proof that it could be done—executing one of my many ideas, that is (☺).

We did as much of the work as we could by ourselves and hired professionals for the bigger tasks. Looking back, it was a great experience, and I am so happy we followed through, but it took a long time and a lot of hard work, assistance, patience, and focused discipline to get the end results. I decided I would need to adopt those same fundamentals in regards to my move. I would need to work hard, have patience, get assistance, and have focused discipline with my time, energy, and money.

Since I had worked for so many years at my job, I had acquired four weeks of paid vacation, and I figured I would use this time as a perfect transition for my move. It was not uncommon for me to take long vacations, as I loved to travel, so planning a four-week sabbatical was not a problem, especially that time of year. In the restaurant business, February is often slow, making it a good time to vacate.

However, in December of 2014, the company I worked for sent out a letter stating a change to their policy in regards to vacation time and pay. It basically changed into an hourly accrual program per time worked rather than a weekly accrual program per year worked. For example, the old policy was work one year and get one week paid vacation, work two years and get two weeks, work three years and get three weeks, and work four years and get four weeks, which was the maximum paid vacation allotted. This was a major incentive to stay with the company. There were many loyal employees who had family in other countries, and they would often work hard for the year and travel back home to visit family during their four-week vacations.

Well, the new program stated that, per hours worked each week, one to five years of work accrued up to one-week paid vacation per year, five to ten years accrued up to two weeks paid vacation, and more than ten years accrued up to four weeks paid vacation. So, for me, who had worked there for just over eight years, this completely changed my vacation benefits. Because I loved to travel, this policy change all of a sudden made the value of working for this company decrease and reaffirmed my decision to move. But, as I've mentioned before, when I want something, I find a way to get it, and I wanted my four weeks of paid vacation. I had earned that time in my eight years. So, discreetly, I worked my magic.

As time pressed on and the finishing touches came together on our house, I began to pack up my things. I started to let a few more people in on my plan, making them promise not to say a word, as I still had a few weeks to finish out at work. I made sure to say my goodbyes to some regular customers, even though some of them simply replied with, "Well, you'll be back in a month."

Only I was to know that that was not the case. I exchanged contact information with a few people and made sure I gave extra big hugs to my elderly guests. At the time, I had estimated I'd spend only nine months to a year on my farm escapades… Little did I know that I would be gone for over two and a half years and that my life would forever be changed.

I eventually dropped the news on Jack. I'd gone over to his house one night for dinner, and we briefly talked about our days. He spent a few minutes venting about his frustrations at work, and I did the same, but when I finished on that topic, I quickly announced, "I'm moving to that farm in Ohio."

"Oh yeah?" he replied with a combination of shock and wonder in a slightly bleak tone. "I feel bad about bitching so much about my day then. That's big news."

I didn't have to explain much after that. I felt ready to go on my journey, ready for change, but telling him still felt…sad. My announcement made it official and marked the end of an era. Although we remained in each other's company for the next few weeks, we drifted apart fairly quickly after that. In fact, the last time I ever spoke with him was the day I pulled out of Reno, and it was only via text. A combination of waving and kiss-face emojis next to the words, "We're on 80!" was all I had in me.

Highway 80 stretched all the way from Reno to St. Louis, Missouri, where we then switched to Interstate 70, which goes straight to Dayton, Ohio. Once in Columbus, you hop on 75 North and *bam*! There you are in Lima, Ohio. Thirty-two hours or so, seven states away, and I was in a whole new world, where grocery clerks want to hear about your evening plans and strangers hold the door open for not only you but the five people behind you as well. This was a place where "Thank you, ma'am" and "Of course, honey" are more commonly heard than not.

I'd left what I knew to explore the great somewhat-unknown. Not soon before I left, I had bumped into my brother's friend Maura at Whole Foods. After an enthusiastic greeting, I inquired about a recent move she had made from Reno to San Francisco.

"This is your comfort zone"—her hands gestured a small circle to the right—"and this is where all the magic happens!" Her hands then moved only slightly to the left and encompassed all of the surrounding areas, as to imply the magic happens everywhere outside of your comfort zone.

This ain't goodbye.
I'm just leaving for now.
I'm walking away,
From all that I know.
I'm taking a leap,
Into the great unknown.
I'm packing the harvest,
Of the seeds that I've sown.
I'm traveling light,
And it's not easy letting go.
This isn't goodbye.
I'm just leaving for now.

Transition

I think I need to backtrack a little because looking back now, it amazes me how many things had to fall into place for this to all work. You see, the timing of my big endeavor just happened to coincide with my mother also planning to move across the country. In 2014, she began to undergo a divorce from her husband. She called me one sunny day in September before my second visit to Ohio, and she asked me if I would drive her and her belongings to Tennessee in order for her to live with her sister once her divorce finalized. She needed to get away for a while, and my aunt just happened to have an extra room and a welcoming heart. I had a truck and the willingness to do anything to help her, so it wasn't a farfetched notion for her to ask this favor of me.

Knowing I would already be across the country with my truck made the idea of moving more tangible. It was only six short hours from my aunt's home in Johnson City, Tennessee, to the farm in Lima, Ohio. And once I had experienced the serene Ohio country life for the second time during the festive fall season, the idea of me actually moving to the farm began to really blossom. I shared the thoughts I had of potentially moving to Ohio with my mother, and we began devising a plan where our plots could unfold together.

"If you can wait for me to get my act together, I will just move to Ohio when you move to Tennessee," I suggested to my mother.

"I don't know if I can wait," she whined. "I need to get out of here—like now!"

"Well, Mom, c'mon. It would be better for us to do this together," I urged.

"Well…" she hesitated. "When could you go? I have to wait until the divorce is finalized anyway," she retorted.

OMG! I thought to myself. *Could this really happen?*

After doing some research, my mother and I bought a trailer in order to haul our belongings some 2,200 miles away. She wanted to take clothes, personal items, jewelry, and her paddleboards and kayak. I was determined to take my California king Tempur-Pedic bed. I had many people attempt to convince me to leave it behind and buy a new bed when I got there, but this nearly brand-new mattress had been given to me from some wonderful friends, so it had sentimental value as well—not to mention I slept like a dad in La-Z-Boy on this thing! Plus, I could never afford to buy another one like it. I refused to live in the basement of a farm and not have amazing sleep for the next year. Besides, we already had the trailer, and the mattress did, in fact, fit inside of it. We just had to finagle a thing…or thirty.

By the time we got my mom's things loaded as well as my all of my personal items, there was hardly room for an extra piece of paper. Thank God for my brother's amazing loading techniques because he somehow managed to squeeze everything in, and we didn't even have to worry it would all come pouring out when the doors were opened. Although when the time came, all of our stuff fit rather well in the trailer, it wasn't long before the actual departure that other challenges arose.

The final details of the transition involved preparing for the major road trip. As the date neared to set forth, my mom's divorce was still not yet finalized, and she realized she was not able to adhere to the timeline to which I had already committed. It was around Christmas in 2014 when my mother actually told me she wouldn't be able to leave in February. Initially, the news was frustrating and had me second-guessing my decision to move.

"Are you kidding me?" I welled up with emotion and devastation as my dream began to unravel in my mind. "So what am I supposed to do now?" I tried to regroup, imagining making the drive solo because I was determined to get to the farm, but I'm not going to lie, I was panic-stricken.

Enter Jill.

My friend Jill and I met during our freshman year of high school. I sat behind her in geometry, and at one point, we were assigned to do a project together. She came over to my parents' house for a sleepover so we could work on our math project, but more importantly, she introduced me to Geto Boys. From then on, we became good friends.

In college, Jill roomed with my oldest brother, Dutney, so naturally, our friendship was easy to keep. Being that she was a good friend of mine as well as my brother's roommate, it wasn't uncommon for Jill to be at a family function or holiday celebration. For graduate school, Jill moved to Florida. Although far apart, we stayed close. Out of all the people I lost touch with over the years, Jill was never one of them. She happened to be home for the holidays and at my house the evening my mom told me she couldn't make the big cross-country trek in February.

"I could drive with you to Ohio," Jill announced in what made my ears ring in angelic harmony. "Road trips with Karissa are the best!" she stated with unreserved excitement.

"Really?" I asked her dead on. "Really!" I began to shout with conviction and hope. "We'd have to, like, really plan this out!"

"Yeah, I mean, I could, like, fly here and drive with you to Ohio and just fly back to Florida," she humbly stated.

"Shut up! Really? You would be down for that?" I was bewildered.

"Well, yeah. You're leaving in February, right? It could be like a birthday road trip!" Jill's birthday was in late February, and mine was in March, so we often planned birthday extravaganzas together.

"OH MY GOD! SHUT UP! I LOVE YOU! REALLY?" I couldn't contain myself. "It will be the best birthday road trip!" I couldn't stop shouting.

This turned out to be the perfect plan, and her sweet mother even offered to chip in on expenses for our journey. The idea of moving across the country had just gotten that much more exciting knowing it would begin with an awesome mission with one of my best friends.

So, there we were, smack dab in the middle of winter, aiming to drive across the country, just two chicks, two dogs, and a truck with a trailer. We gave ourselves seven days to make the drive, but we ended up doing it in five. There was a major ice storm spreading across the US at the time. We didn't care. We were fearless. We were ambitious. And, most importantly, we were together. We made sure to equip ourselves with plenty of warm clothes, snacks, and whiskey for the late-night hotel arrivals.

We made it to Provo, Utah, the first night on the road—of course, not before stopping at In-N-Out burger on our way out of Reno. Later, I would long for many of my hometown familiarities, like that first perfectly crunchy, savory bite of a double double.

We wanted to make the most of our drive by seeing some national parks and US landmarks along the way. Our first major goal was to hit Arches National Park in Utah. We spent a few hours the first day exploring, hiking, and taking pictures in the desert, where our dark clothes stood out against the tan sand like an oil stain on concrete. Our spirits were lifted by the awe of the natural landscape of these formations that were centuries old.

On the second night of our road trip, we attempted to stay with a high school friend in Denver. Unfortunately, that fell through, so we resorted to a handy app called Hotel Tonight that allowed us to find a nearby, affordable hotel at 11:00 p.m. The third day, we hit the road early and didn't experience much excitement as we moseyed our way through what we thought was the flattest, most boring state in the US: Kansas. That day, we were determined not to stop until we couldn't drive any farther. We had made it just past St. Louis when we pulled in to a La Quinta Inn, utterly exhausted.

"Where's the whiskey?" I asked Jill.

"In the trailer," she said as we looked at each other, knowing what a chore it would be to dig up. Our hesitation was brief though, and our eye contact and mutual facial expressions affirmed we were ready to tackle the mission of finding it. We had just driven all day and night for Pete's sake! We needed to celebrate.

I opened the trailer's side door, and instantly, my belongings we'd shoved in last minute came spilling out. As I tried to keep my things from hitting the ground, Jill popped her head in with a flashlight so she could begin the Wild Turkey hunt. Did I mention it was freezing outside? We could see our breaths in the cold, and we shivered as we stood in the parking lot, underdressed and unkempt, desperately searching the trailer for the bottle.

"I found it!" Jill shouted.

"Yay!" I agreed with enthusiasm and relief. "I'm freezing!" I added with urgency and intention.

"Me too. Let's go drink ourselves a blanket!" Jill excitedly announced.

And that we did.

The next night, we stayed with a friend in the middle of nowhere, Cornland, Illinois. His name was Aaron Michael Davis, but I called him AMD for short. I had met him a couple of years prior at Yosemite National Park when my friend Taylor and I were standing in front of a trailhead sign that had a map of the trail on it. We studied the map as we plotted our course for the hike the following day. AMD happened to be doing the same thing at that same moment in time. Being the oh-so-social and friendly butterfly that I am, we got to chitchatting with this fellow wilderness lover, and we agreed we'd see each other on the trail the next day. From that moment on, we began an adventure-filled friendship.

Later in the same year we met, AMD flew back out West to go to Yosemite again and hike Half Dome with a group of us. My brother and I put him up at our house. It was during that time that he extended the offer with his polite, country-twanged voice, "If ya'll are ever in my neck of the woods, I'll return the favor."

*Yeah, like we'd ever be in your neck of the woods…*or so I thought.

Some two years later and I was eating my own words and needing a free place to stay in the middle of Nowhere, USA. Who'd have thought we would take him up on his offer? And not only did he let us stay at his house, but he let us have his room, and his mother even brought over fresh linens! There's just something so welcoming about country folk.

After briefly getting settled at his place, AMD took us out for a night on the one-stoplight town to a local eatery where everybody literally knew everybody, and they also knew we weren't from the area. When we walked in the doors, we were introduced to the eight or ten patrons scattered throughout the joint. AMD announced to the curious onlookers that we were a couple Western girls just passing through. That little po-dunk town offered us a warm welcome as we relaxed into the scene of the bar. We ordered chicken tenders, some whisky for Jill, and a Coors Light for me, which mildly set us apart from the Miller Lite sipping crowd. Different strokes for different folks, I suppose. Since we were feeling pretty spent from our travels, we filled our bellies and enjoyed the carefree milieu of the short-lived evening. We made our way back to our humble, temporary abode to get some rest.

The next morning, AMD announced, "I have a surprise for you!"

He insisted that he make us his famous egg-hole breakfast sandwiches. He cheerfully walked us through each step as we sluggishly relaxed on his couch and enjoyed the hospitality of being in a loving home.

"First, you cut a hole in the center of two slices of bread…" he attempted to teach us as if we were paying close attention. His energy level was far higher than ours at that time.

"Then, ya fry an egg in each hole," he continued. "And then, you gotta melt the cheese on one half and fry up some sliced ham for the other half." He was so enthusiastic. "Then, ya slap 'em together so it's just right." AMD stared at the masterpieces he concocted for the three of us, and they didn't disappoint. It was the perfect send-off breakfast.

The last leg of our trek was almost seamless. By trial and error, Jill and I eventually learned which states didn't sell alcohol at convenience stores. We were bound and determined not to show up to the farm empty-handed, and we ended up on some two-hour detour in search of another bottle of Wild Turkey. *Oh bother,* I thought to myself in Eeyore's distressed voice as we hunted.

Needless to say, we didn't show up emptyhanded. We made memories, we had fun, and most importantly, we made it safely to Ohio. When we finally pulled into the farm on the evening of February 27, my truck's thermometer illuminated a number I had never seen on its screen before: a bright green negative 9°F.

What the hell did I just get myself in to? I wondered.

"We're here! We're here! We made it!" I screamed with excitement.

"Dogs, we're here! This is your new home!" Jill announced as the dogs woke from their cross-country travel coma.

As we peeled our legs off the seats and shut off the roar of the diesel engine, we stepped out into the darkness of night. There was one outdoor light on above the garage, but the atmosphere was otherwise dark and dormant. Our rural location allowed the stars to illuminate in the sky like a blanket of white string lights; the bright reflection of the moon upon the snow-covered lands whispered wonderful words of excitement and awe to my soul. *This* was my new home.

The Pub

Ahh, the pub ☺.

There's nothing quite like the friendly atmosphere of your neighborhood watering hole. For the east side of the small city of Lima, Ohio, the Elm Tree Pub provided just that. The antique wooden bar set the stage for this quality establishment. This particular feature was restored decades before from a barn on a nearby farm and did not move from its location, nestled in the back of this restaurant, throughout the many business endeavors that occupied the building over the years.

An old, heavy, metal-handled door projected confidence and comfort and provided a welcoming entrance into the Elm Tree Pub. A small breezeway with a vibrant Roger Blanchon painting of a hectic kitchen scene hanging on the southern wall housed a greeting spot for those coming and going. Once inside, the cheerful and professional staff offered pleasant greetings. The walls of the establishment were adorned with eclectic pieces of art and meaningful pictures from different eras. On the first page of the Pub's menu was a story that told the life of the bar and all of the people who had made it what it is today.

Hello, friends! Have you noticed me behind the bar? I am one of the oldest bars in the area, dating back to the early 1900s when I was a permanent fixture at the Old Mill Saloon on Lima's Main Street. Thirsty patrons would arrive by horse and buggy and belly up to the bar for a shot of whisky or other legal libations. As Ohio entered the prohibition era, I served less intoxicating Coca-Cola and lemonade. Perhaps these non-alcoholic beverages weren't as popular as whiskey, because I was involuntarily moved into storage. In 1936, local resident Darnell Davis discovered me in a barn in Lafayette, and I soon became part of the new Davis' Restaurant at this Elm Tree location. Over the next forty-six years, I made so many friends and was always around whenever anyone needed me. In 1982, Bob and Patty Thorn adopted me and my home and reopened as Thorn's Restaurant. I served fewer libations during that time and more home-cooked meals. In 2002, the Wescott family took me in and renamed the place Wes's Diner. It was so nice to see our guests rush in for Wes's famous corn cakes. After working nonstop for seventy-seven years, I finally was able to take a rest for a few years. Then one day, I heard footsteps in the kitchen. It was John and Jamie Galt. They fell in love with me and wanted to bring me back to life. They even hooked me up with a hot new front bar. We make a great pair, don't you think? I feel good enough to go another 100 years. I must say, I am having a great time rekindling old relationships and making so many new ones. So, welcome to the Elm Tree Pub, where it really is all about me!

Cheers!

On my twenty-seventh birthday, I went to the pub for a celebratory drink with my new roommates, Annie and Olivia. We dined and drank and enjoyed our newfound friendships. I had officially lived in Ohio for just over two weeks at this point, and the bond in our household was in the early stages of development, but dining and drinking together would become a regular part of our sisterhood.

This was my third Elm Tree Pub experience. At the first dinner, with Annie and some of her friends a few weeks prior, the seed was planted for me to apply for a job. I actually filled out an application then and there and had a brief interview with Jamie, one of the owners, at the very table where the group dined. The second visit was when I came in for a formal interview with the general manager and got a little more acquainted with the place. And on my birthday, my third visit to the establishment, Jamie brought over four Scorned Women (their house shot made of pepper-infused vodka and mango puree), and while also wishing me a happy birthday, she excitedly welcomed me to the Elm Tree Pub crew! The four of us cheered and tossed back those cool yet fiery shots. Things had continued to unfold beautifully for me in Ohio, but without the pub, many connections would have never been formed.

John and Jamie took me in not only as an employee but also as a friend. From the get-go, they respected my dreams to learn about farming and my ambitions of being solo on an enterprise in Ohio, and they communicated and worked with me to have a mutually beneficial relationship. Although we lived in Lima, they quickly encouraged me to go to Columbus for some bigger city fun. It wasn't long before they took me out to some local restaurants and bars in downtown Columbus to show me a different perspective of Ohio. This time was priceless and irreplaceable to me.

Since I was used to Reno, and the goings on of a somewhat bigger city than Lima, with a population of approximately 30,000 people, I was excited to be introduced to Columbus, that had almost a million residents and nearly fifty colleges in the area. The city-life Columbus offered resonated with me a little more than the country-life I'd enlisted with on the farm, and I think the Galts detected this once they got to know me. They were both from Ohio, so they knew the sweet spots.

Jamie gave me the nickname "Nevada," and it didn't take long for this name to catch on. She said she got the idea from the movie *Coyote Ugly* because they nicknamed a newly hired bartender from New Jersey "Jersey." I loved it. I loved how quickly my new employers took to me and vice versa. They embraced me as a young woman on an adventure to an unfamiliar part of the country.

I loved to watch John and Jamie together. They were a perfect example of passionate love. It was obvious they adored each other and also that they respected and cared for one another. By working for them, I was able to see how their level of communication and ambition worked in their favor. Their business was a success, and although they spent many hours working it, they worked it together. They had complementary skills and a genuine love that seemed to radiate from them, each as individuals and also together as a couple.

The Galts were both in their forties. Jamie had a friendly and vivacious spunk to her. She wore her bright red hair short and had a thin, athletic build. She was all woman with her attire and demeanor. John came off as the serious and meticulous businessman, but he had a familiar smile and sense of community that fueled his restaurant endeavor. I later learned of his free spirit and passion for music when he told me that he was a Dead Head, a term used to describe the loyal fanbase of the band the Grateful Dead. I loved how you could feel their personalities all throughout their business—the smiles, hugs, and handshakes given to each guest and an impressive use of patron names. It was like working at *Cheers*, and I ate up every minute of it.

John and Jamie appeared to be inseparable. It was uncommon to see one without the other, and more often than not, they were holding hands, exchanging kisses, or engaging in conversations with others as a conjoined duo. I would watch them as they executed running a business built from love, and I would think to myself how I wanted what they had. I wanted a hardworking, loving partner who had complementary traits and was passionate, dedicated, and focused.

Working at the pub sure showed me how much different a bar in Lima, Ohio, was from where I worked in Reno, Nevada. One of the differences I noticed was in the style of the Midwest country folk. I wouldn't say that anyone talked with too much of a Southern drawl or anything, but conversations were laid back, welcoming, and at times, pleasantly simple. People would kindly ask questions about me, my life, or even just my day, and they would genuinely care and want to hear what I had to say. Their stories were slow-paced, and they had a less-to-the-point type of conversation, a result from what, I think, was a combination of the good-natured people, manners, and the way they were raised. And I loved their idioms. "Well, that just dill's my pickle," and "I haven't heard that in a coon's age," or "Well, you believe I'll fix her wagon" (and I'm pretty sure there was no actual wagon that needed a fixin') were some of my favorites.

Along with their age-old phrases, Ohio is definitely a state where generations have their legacies. Most folks either live with, near, or not far from their parents, grandparents, aunts, uncles, cousins, children, and grandchildren. I have met and envied so many people who are so geographically close to their families. Now, I'm not saying relationally close (to each their own on that matter), but most people from Ohio stay in Ohio. And, from what I learned, most of those who do move away, eventually move back.

I was 2,200 miles away from my family, and if I think about it, I've never in my life even lived in the same 300-mile radius of any of my distant relatives. So you can imagine why I soaked up the opportunity to meet new people and hear stories of their family dynamics; it was all so unfamiliar to me, and I suppose I was unfamiliar to them.

"Why in God's name would you move from Reno to Lima, Ohio?" This was the most commonly asked question I got—in one form or another. Most people were downright shocked to hear I *chose* to move to the middle of the "Buckeye State" as opposed to having been dragged by family or circumstance.

After being asked this so many times, I eventually developed a streamlined answer. But at first, I would tell people I moved to Ohio to learn about farming. I had the family members of a dear friend and mentor of mine welcome me to come live with and learn from them. I'd explain that I grew up riding horses, yet I lived in the city, and my family was in no way related to or interested in the country life. I'd express my experience in the kitchen and my curiosities to know more about where food comes from. But that turned into a mouthful quickly, so I'd eventually just sum it all up and say I came to do an internship on a cattle farm. It didn't take me long to realize that short answer would drive my point home and save me from repeating the same ten-minute spiel about how I ended up where I was.

Let me just say, I loved my role as a bartender there at the Elm Tree Pub. In a new place with new surroundings, it was nice to find myself in a bit of a comfort zone, and it wasn't long before I had my regular shifts with familiar-faced patrons sitting opposite the bar top from me. Some of them grew up on farms, so we often shared stories of the experiences we now had in common. Some people confessed to me they ran away from farm life. The agonizing work of being up before the sun to go to a stockyard sale or to bale hay scarred them. I lived for these conversations, for the conversations that made me look at life and people differently, for conversations that resulted in friendships.

I worked at the pub part-time for about a year, and over that time, I met Randy. He was a well-known guest at the pub. He was maybe in his late forties or early fifties, and he would come in alone, with friends, or with his children at least once a week—if not more. He drank

Woodford on the rocks with a splash of water; on occasion, he would order a double. He sure could put them away. He was a good-natured, smart, hard-working business owner, and before long, we became well acquainted. Eventually, we got to talking about my desire to learn to bow hunt. It was on my list of things to seriously learn while in Ohio. I had this wild fantasy that I would kill a deer while riding a horse. (Hey, if you're gonna dream, dream big!) Randy was a hunter himself, and he told me about a target range set up out behind his work shed. He told me how his friends and sons would come over periodically to have a cookout and practice shooting their bows.

After learning of this truth, we would touch base on that topic quite often. One day when I arrived at work, Randy was sitting there at the bar, and he told me he had a surprise for me.

"Uh-oh, do I even want to know?" I asked with a slight grimace on my face.

"You're going to love it!" he replied with great enthusiasm. "I'll go get it!"

"Oh boy. Here we go," I said, looking over at the other bartender who was just about to leave after finishing her shift.

I carried on with my duties of getting my coworker out of there and getting the bar set up for my shift. I counted the cash register and made sure the money was correct for the day. I checked the coolers to see what I might need to stock and then started doing my rounds with open checks for the other guests at the bar. I saw Randy walk back in with almost a skip in his step and a huge grin on his face.

"Well…" I asked, noticing he was empty-handed. I was not sure what he was up to at this point.

"It's over by the door," he said, motioning his head

toward the entrance of the restaurant, which hid around the corner from the bar. I eagerly and with slight annoyance walked around to see what this surprise was all about.

"AH! SHUT UP! OH MY GOD!" I screamed as I realized what was propped up behind the hostess stand. "Are you kidding me?! What is this?"

Luckily, there weren't too many people in the building at the time because I sure made a fuss about it. But, oh my gosh, there it was—a green camouflage Hoyt Ignite bow leaning up against the wall. It was accented with pink letters, clearly designed for a female. I was uncertain and a little bit in shock when I tried to wrap my mind around the idea that someone I was merely acquainted with would bring in a bow as a surprise for me.

He didn't get up from his seat as I walked back around the corner and demanded in a high-pitched voice, "What is that?!"

"That's your new bow," he replied simply with a genuine smirk.

"No way! I can't accept this! That's an expensive bow!" I replied.

"Well, my buddy got it for his wife, and when he found out she was cheating on him, he decided not to give it to her, and when I told him how excited you were about learning to hunt, he sold it to me for a real good price."

"Oh my gosh, Randy! No, you can't just buy me a bow."

"Well, yes, I can, and I did."

"Let me pay you for it. Oh my gosh! It's so beautiful!"

I'm not sure purchasing a bow was on the top of my financial to-do list at that point, even though learning to hunt was on my Ohio to-do list, but Randy's generosity opened my world to a whole new realm of focus and pursuit. Plus, living on the farm made it extremely easy and accessible for me to get acquainted with the sport.

Within a couple weeks, Randy introduced me to his brother-in-law who just happened to have a business as an archery instructor. He then set me up with a private session that included a full day of setting up my bow and learning to shoot at an indoor range as well as a few hours on an outdoor, life-sized animal target field. In addition to this kickass experience, my instructor also offered me eight custom arrows made right before my eyes. That single day introduced me to a side of myself I never knew existed. I was enthralled, and according to my target practice, I was also a natural. The bull's-eyes and kill shots spoke for themselves.

I couldn't believe where I was in my life. I was doing things I had only thought about and all because I had awesome employers who took me under their wings and incredible bar patrons who provided me with opportunity and encouragement. Above all, I understood at a different level what it felt like to be cared for.

Happenings

I'd say the first couple months or so of being in Ohio were filled with me eagerly searching for whatever opportunities I could find. Since I was the new girl on the farm, I was often invited to join activities from the individual members of the group. I met mutual friends and various family members of the bunch rather frequently. I was delighted by the gratifying acceptance I received at every turn. It appeared that, other than Bruce, the father of the farm, the family was rather social. I enjoyed this immensely because I too was a social being and moving to a farm in the middle of Ohio could have proven to be very isolating. To my surprise, there were many opportunities to mix and mingle in the community.

It seemed that almost every day, someone would graciously invite me to do something. I got to partake in events both large and small. I went cross-country skiing, attended a farmer's conference, tapped maple trees for syrup sap, donated blood, and played the fifth wheel on double dates with Annie, her boyfriend, and their friends. Olivia invited me to art viewings and delicious dinners with acquaintances in the area. I would occasionally escort Bee and her daughter Deborah to the farmers' markets. And Cindy never hesitated to invite me to local live music shows and to meet her friends who shared similar free spirits. I jubilantly said yes to pretty much every offer that came my way. I was aiming to change my priorities from having a structured plan about what to do with my time to going with the flow, letting the wind that blew upon my open, beseeching shore take me.

Through this time, I was introduced to other members of the caste. One dear soul, Rachel, was Annie's cousin on her father's side of the family; she was also one of Annie's best friends. Rachel eventually took me on mini-adventures and daytrips to see special spots of the Central Ohio Valley that were off the tourist-beaten path. Over coffee and conversation, we grew to be close friends rather quickly. She was just a few years older than me and worked as a substitute teacher. She had dreams of owning a gift shop, and she also shared a passion for writing. She was full of warmth and love, and we connected on a deep spiritual level through our exchanges about the hardships we'd both endured in our pasts. We shared a similar curiosity to some of life's bigger questions. Over time, I found great comfort in our friendship, and I loved that she too shared close relationships with the people I was beginning to call family.

Excursion by excursion, person by person, I eventually started to become a part of their tribe. I felt connected and accepted without uncertainty. The group would gather on a regular basis, sometimes the whole gang and sometimes just two or three of them would meet up. Religiously, Cindy would drive to her friend Claire's house on Thursdays after her evening yoga class. Claire lived on the shoreline of a nearby lake called Grand Lake. She and Cindy would kayak into the sunset-filled horizon, paddling away their worries and soaking in the fresh air and comradery. It wasn't long before I was making this a regular event in my week as well. Since I had my paddleboard with me among the belongings I toted across the country, I jumped at the opportunity to use it. I loved going to Claire's for an evening of bonding, sweating, and chumming it up on the water, knowing there was a refreshing cocktail reward waiting for us afterward.

Claire was in her forties with two teenage children. She was divorced, owned her own business, and from what I could tell, had a divine creative force that ferociously existed through her being. She was a type A personality. She had a generous heart, witty mind, and hilarious sense of humor. She was always conjuring up some incredible scheme to win the hearts of her employees, clients, and friends. She was also a freakishly talented artist; she could draw, paint, sew, write, sing, decorate, and host a party like no other! I was drawn to her presence like a moth to a light. I wanted to befriend this wonderful woman and learn how to replicate the sense of ease she emitted in her existence. She showed her fondness for my exemplary culinary skills, and before long, our friendship too blossomed. How was I so lucky to meet so many special people? I often asked myself. I couldn't have dreamt of a more perfect place to call home.

Cindy was an inspirational woman who was well connected to her community. I went to her studio for reviving yoga classes twice a week. She would often trade me the cost of a class for some chores around the farm, which was a perk for me since I was still getting settled financially. She invited me to check out a book club and sewing group that she was a part of so I could continue to meet new faces and learn the lay of the land.

Though we all had things in common, I think Cindy, Claire, and I really bonded when we went to an annual poetry event held at the Lodge in the Hocking Hills. They'd given me a heads up on the event, so I entered a demure poem to the contest, which was lavishly blown out of the water when I heard the winning contestants of the event read their poems. But still, I had made it my mission to eagerly participate in anything and everything full speed ahead, and I held no regrets or reservations.

And I mean it when I say I didn't turn down opportunities. I found myself helping cater one woman's son's graduation party and another family asked if I could feed their baby lambs while they were away for a long weekend. I loved saying yes to everything, and the little bit of extra cash didn't hurt either. I wanted to engage, I wanted to be involved, and I wanted to continue to expand my network. After all, if I hadn't said yes to joining Jim on my initial visit, I would have never been where I was. I took each proposal as a chance to open doors for my future, although sometimes I would accept an invitation as merely a chance to sit back, unwind, and be a wall fly for a while.

Not long after my arrival, I accompanied Annie, Thomas, and his girlfriend to a local dive bar that offered twenty-five-cent wings. It was only about fifteen minutes away, and this hole in the wall wasn't much to write home about, but there was something about the way the country music played over the jukebox that made this place work.

As I sat with Annie and Thomas, I started to feel like I was part of an entourage. This sibling duo was like a pair of celebrities, and nearly every person in the joint knew them. One by one, or even three by three, people would approach us, they'd share a few minutes of banter, I'd be introduced, and the passersby would fall back into the oblivion of the bar. I met a good deal of country folk that night and enjoyed observing the patrons in their cozy environment as the clamor grew louder with each hour that passed.

In one of our many conversations in the bar, Annie and I touched on the topic of raising chickens. She told me about some research she had been doing and asked if I would like to be involved. Well, that was a no-brainer: Heck yes! Of course, I wanted to help! She told me she wanted to go look at a coop she'd found for sale online and that she planned to order chicks from her childhood friend that worked at a feed mill. I was ecstatic! Within a week, the "tres bitches," as we so proudly called ourselves at SP, were the new mammas of a dozen baby chicks. We named them all with specific hilarity and joked about our favorites: Easter Candy, Aunt Jemima, and Duck. There was a catch though. They needed to live indoors since it was so cold outside in the middle of March. So where did they live? None other than the Nevada suite! (aka, the basement).

It was about this same time that Olivia got a phone call from an acquaintance who knew that she lived on a farm and had a heart for animals. The call was to say there were two lambs that were orphaned and needed a home. So, within a ten-day period, we had a dozen baby chicks and two tiny lambs living at the Sinner's Palace. We named the lambs Shishka and Bob—their fate was inevitable. It was all too perfect. Since I lived in the basement quarters that had a utility room connected to my bathroom, I got to have first-hand experience on raising infant animals. Chirping noises and baas were commonly heard throughout the wee hours of most nights. Boy, was I feeling like a farmer now! The lambs needed to be bottle-fed every four hours, and well, the chicks were messy and clever little shits. But honestly, I ate up every second of it. It was a hoot having them live in the basement with me, and it sure gave me a story to tell!

Among the enjoyable chaos at home, I was still exploring the Ohio area for opportunities to earn money and determine my new routine. Thanks to Craigslist, I answered an ad for another part-time job in the big city of Columbus. I simply wanted to make money and meet people, so I figured it would be fun to branch out into the city as well. Many people from the country commuted to Columbus for work, so the idea didn't seem too far-fetched. I applied for a part-time serving job at a restaurant in a giant outdoor mall that served as a hub for the Central Ohio area. It was about an hour away from the farm, and although I knew the drive would be a pain in the ass, I also was convinced it would be cool to dip my toes in the waters of a bigger city. As it turned out, when I went in for an interview at the place I'd applied, there was a much more intriguing restaurant across the street that called my attention.

I walked over and was greeted by a tall, handsome, clean-cut, dark-haired man wearing a very formal uniform with a white collared shirt, dark green vest, and white apron that nearly touched the floor. He asked if I wanted a table, and I told him I was actually inquiring if they were hiring. He took me to a high top in the fancy bar area and asked me to wait while he went to speak with the manager. It must have been my lucky day because the manager on duty happened to be a big fan of Reno and that connection gave me an in. He was on the National Bowling League that held its annual event in Reno, and I thank this factoid for the events that followed.

I had plenty of experience working in a steakhouse, and I did look pretty cute that day. Everyone who interviewed me was a male, so I think that worked to my advantage. They offered me a position as a food runner and said that it was no problem for me to only work two shifts a week; they even said I could work a double-shift in one day so I didn't have to make the commute as often. Why in the world would they offer me such a convenient schedule? I didn't ask. I didn't care. And I was hired then and there.

My time was spread around the various places I'd committed to. I worked sparingly on the farm when they needed me and especially if there was an opportunity to learn or experience something new; Annie always made sure to include me in the exciting events. I worked at the pub a few nights a week as my steady stream of income, and I worked at the steakhouse, usually on the weekends for one or two days.

While getting into the groove of my new life, Olivia told me she would be house-sitting for a friend in Columbus, and she offered for me to stay with her overnight when she heard I had to work late at the steakhouse and return again the next morning at 10:30 a.m. This proved to be a blessing because juggling the multiple facets of my scattered schedule was starting to catch up to me, and the hour-plus commute each way didn't help. I realized this was exactly what I had signed up for, but we all need to refuel sometimes, and I was running on empty.

I arrived to the house around midnight, and Olivia graciously let me in, giving me brief instructions to make sure I closed the door completely and locked it so the scheming animals couldn't escape; you know, the old "lock the door handle, not the deadbolt routine." She showed me where the coffee pot was and the room where I would be staying, and since she had to be up at six in the morning, we briefly exchanged hugs and tiresome comments and then she quickly went off to bed. I was so excited to have a few extra hours to sleep, write, and get some much-needed Facebook time in before heading off for a short drive to work at my relatively new job the next morning.

The next morning, I arose with ease and made my way to the kitchen for a delicious cup of brew, investigating the house for a cozy nook where I could settle in with my journal. I was excited to have a rather effortless morning.

Before I could begin writing, however, I remembered I had left my work clothes and iPad in my truck the night before in a sleepy haze. Wearing barely there shorts and a small tank top as pajamas, which seemed appropriate for a Nevada-to-Ohio transplant during the late-spring's humidity, I took one sip of my piping hot coffee, set it on the nightstand, and walked out to my truck to grab my work shirt and iPad. I pulled the door shut behind me as to not allow the cats or dog to follow me out, but as I heard the sound of the door close—*Click*—I instantly regretted my decision. Yep, you guessed it. I locked myself out, but this wasn't just a typical "Shoot, I left my car keys in the car while I went into the grocery store" kind of lock out. This was the mother of all lock outs, the "I'm in Ohio on a journey of exploration, so I'm going to do everything at 150%" kind of lock out. Let's recap: I'm practically naked on the front porch of a stranger's house, alone, and with no phone and no way directly contact anyone I knew personally in the middle of Ohio with only a few hours to spare before I'm supposed to be at my new job.

I assessed my situation and attempted to find an open window or hidden key. Without success, I realized I was probably going to need some help, but there was no way I was going to go banging on doors scantily clad. I only imagined what a neighbor would think if they saw me half-dressed trying to break into this home. I didn't even know the names of the people who lived there! And trust me, I easily looked like I was up to no good. I did, however, have my truck keys in hand, so luckily, I was able to grab a passable garment out of my truck-closet and cover the top half of my body. *This is as good as it's going to get...* I mustered up as much of my dignity as I could and started walking...barefoot.

Down the street, I was excited to see a neighbor's garage door open, and when I realized the man was vacuuming his car, I hoped to get his attention. When he noticed that I was standing in his driveway, he turned off the vacuum to acknowledge me. I bashfully explained my situation to the man in hopes for assistance. Raymond, the sweet eighty-or-so-years-old African American man, offered his phone and a friendly suggestions as to how to resolve my situation.

"Why don't yous try the Facebook?" he kindly suggested.

Genius! I thought, *Duh, why didn't I think of that?*

Having not memorized ANY Ohio phone numbers, I relied on Google and Facebook to navigate me back to my delicious, what would now be warm at best, cup of coffee that my heart so longed for.

By this time, it was about 9:30, and I realized I would surely be late for my 10:30 shift. Using sweet Ray's phone, I looked up all of the phone numbers I could think of that might lead me to a solution: the restaurant, the farm, the grandparents, the Lord himself. Without seconds in between dials, I called anyone I could think of for help.

"Helloooo? Is anyone there? Please pick up!" The desperation in my voice was almost comical. "It's Karissa. Hello? Oh no, no, no, no, no, nooooo. I need heelllpp! Please pick up the phone!" I pleaded on the farm's answering machine to no avail. I attempted to call the restaurant to inform them of my trials, but there too was no answer. I left a vague message that I would be late, and I trembled with anxiety because it was only like my third or fourth weekend working there, and I wasn't sure if my charm factor had kicked in yet. I could feel the tension rising within me as Ray's wife repeatedly peered out the door to see who I was and what was going on.

It became obvious that I had outstayed my neighborly welcome in Ray's garage. Since he had to get going with his day, he respectfully supplied me a pen and paper to write directions to Olivia's' work office, which was about a half hour away. Fortunately, she had her position and company name on her Facebook profile, because I surely couldn't recall it. I googled the phone number and address still using the kind man's phone. The last call I made on Ray's phone was to her office, but the phone operating hours were only Monday through Friday and, of course, it was Saturday. I posted a Facebook post to her wall, but I didn't receive a reply within the confines of my time limit with the stranger's phone in hand. So, it was determined: off I would go, into a city I was unfamiliar with, to a place I wasn't sure of its location, in hopes that my pile of lemons would produce some thirst-quenching lemonade.

My emotions were welled up within me so great that I just burst into laughter. I hopped in my truck, turned up the tunes, rolled down the windows, and put my pedal to the metal. I was still trying to race the clock so I could make it to my shift just a little late, but I began to realize my predicament was getting the best of me. Then, out of the corner of my eye, I saw a flash of my roommate driving down the main, traffic-filled road, heading in the opposite direction. I quickly busted a U-turn in an effort to chase down this little white car! It turned out my mind was tormented with the effect of having a lack of caffeine, and to my disillusion, it was not her, and I was, in fact, chasing down a stranger. Sad face. So, now what?

I looked to my left and saw a beautiful ray of light shining on the gorgeous and familiar green and white sign of a Starbucks. I pulled in so that I could regain my composure and get some java fuel. I scurried around my truck, looking for enough change to purchase a satiable remedy. I stumbled into the coffeeshop, looking rather dapper and unfrazzled in my Nevada's finest outfit and beyond thankful no one in this city knew what an entrepreneur of Fourth Street in Reno looked like. I modestly stood in line and plotted my next step.

However, being the chatty Cathy that I am, it wasn't long before I made a friend in line, to whom I shared my pitiful situation, and he offered his phone and brain to help my cause. I checked my Facebook, and thank the heavens Olivia had replied! I asked her for her phone number, and she replied instantly! The friendly gentleman allowed me to use his phone to call her, and I was able to get more accurate directions to her place of business, which I apparently needed because she said the building was locked on the weekends and she would not have seen me at all had I come without her knowing. I called my work and apologetically notified them I would be extremely late! I was two for two as far as friendly assistants went, and I asked the kind sir what I could do to thank him. He replied, "Just have a great day!"

As I drove the half hour to pick up the house key, I pondered his polite response. *Just have a great day. Just have a great day.* I made the decision to do just that. So what if I was late to work! So what if I just trekked across a foreign town in my underwear! There are worse things that could happen. I could have been fired, but I wasn't. I could have forgotten my car keys inside and been doubly locked out, but I wasn't. Sweet Ray and my new Starbucks friend could have ignored me, but they didn't. This was a hiccup, a minor inconvenience, and I'd be lying if I didn't say it was pretty freaking funny in hindsight.

I made the drive back to the house, threw some ice in my original cup of coffee, got ready for work, and made it there only two hours late! (Ha!) Needless to say, I had a day. But that was just it. It was just a day.

Annette

What charges and drains your life battery?

The answers to this question for me at the time revolved around intentionally surrounding myself with people and experiences that attracted the eyes of my heart. I valued hard work. I valued authenticity. I valued good-natured people and genuine connection. I valued laughing and making people laugh. I valued learning, especially hands-on. I valued exposing myself to the unknown and filling in the blanks of my imagination with truths that I yearned to explore. But above all, I valued shenanigans!

I was first introduced to Annette when I flew back to Ohio for my second visit to the Reynolds' farm. She was blonde, her features easy on the eyes. Her complexion was flawless, and the expression on her faced never changed. She stood all of three feet tall, and well, she was made of plastic. You see, Annette was a doll from Annie's childhood, and on her thirtieth birthday, her mother, Cindy, dug Annette out from the attic and decided to reintroduce the beloved toy at the party they had. Boy, did this treasure become a target for jokes and pranks for years to come.

By the time I was living in Ohio, there had already been a few jokes starring Annette being passed around the farm. I only knew the tales secondhand, but the first involved Annie's roommate hanging Annette from the ceiling with a noose around her neck and a chair toppled below her feet. This might seem morbid to the layman, but the twisted sense of humor that everyone shared made this shenanigan fit the bill. For the next bit, Annie's brother, Thomas, placed a shotgun in the lap of Annette while she sat on the couch. When Annie arrived home from work, she was met with hysterical laughter by the sight of this doll prepared to protect the home. For the next practical joke, sometime later, Annette found herself in the bathroom during another party with a Pepto-Bismol bottle next to her, chocolate smeared around her mouth, and a plate of cookies by the sink. She was positioned as if to be hurling into the toilet, and needless to say, it was a hilarious hit in the eyes of the partygoers.

When I was formally introduced to Annette and told of the shenanigans, I couldn't wait to be involved. Since it was during my second visit to Ohio that I met this doll, I didn't know the family too terribly well at this point, but I was eager to partake in creative plots to contribute to the fun. One evening, Annie and I wanted to sneak Annette into Cindy's yoga studio after hours to surprise her when she showed up to teach the next morning. We felt the rush of adrenaline as we peered over our shoulders and hurried to keep our ploy covert as we carried Annette, not-so-discreetly wrapped in a blanket, and entered through the backdoor after the midnight hour. To our pleasure, the joke worked marvelously, and it actually scared Cindy when she saw what she thought was a child laid out on a mat on the wooden floor of the studio. She later told us her students got a real kick out of it that morning as well. Mission accomplished!

Although these antics would often occur months apart from one another, each occasion brought a synergistic connection to the group that would only grow our bond as a whole. Each stunt seemed to somehow outdo the last, and Annette seemed to enjoy her many charades: being dressed up for the holidays, participating in pumpkin-carving parties, serving as the angel on the Christmas tree, and lounging by the pool in her favorite two-piece bathing suit. When my mother came to visit, she even took it upon herself to dress Annette up as an old lady with costume jewelry and antique glasses and place her on a chair near the fireplace with a book in her hand and a couple mini bottles of vodka in her lap. The jokes seemed to keep coming, and each time, no matter what the case, the figurine brought a lighthearted joy to everyone's hearts.

When I worked at the steakhouse, our gang of girls planned to come in for Claire's birthday, and we couldn't wait to sneak Annette into the Wine Room, which was a private dining room in the wine cellar of the restaurant. Annie dressed her up in dominatrix fashion—black whip and fishnet stockings included—and we positioned her spread-eagle around an oversized bottle of champagne on a high shelf in the room. We could barely get through the dinner because each time she caught one of our eyes, the entire table lost it. Claire proudly toted Annette out of the fancy place, tears in her eyes from all the laughter.

With examples such as the adventures of Annette, it was easy for me to quickly fall in love with the new community I found myself in. Not only was I having the time of my life making comical memories, but I was also really coming to understand the life of a farmer. As one might imagine, being a farmer is filled with constant setbacks and hardships. After all, farming is running a business highly dependent on the weather and the health of the people working it. Since this was a family operation, the Reynolds' lives were intertwined with each other in pretty much every aspect of life. They would have regular morning meetings, usually at headquarters, and throughout the day, they would communicate with each other their priorities and most urgent tasks. More often than not, something would arise that would need to be tended to, sometimes by everyone. In addition to their personal desires, appointments, social events, and family matters, the all-too-common, yet unexpected rainstorms would force many efforts to be delayed, or worse, redone when the weather cleared. But they did it, and they did it with grace—far more grace and patience than I ever knew was possible. And I was so blessed that this family invited me along for the firsthand and special ride.

Since my days were jam-packed with to-dos and events that seemingly happened so fast, I quickly learned that it would benefit me to document major events on my phone when I didn't have a journal handy. I didn't want to miss a detail of this journey, and I greatly valued being able to document occurrences in a moment's notice.

A note from the Notes App:

> *This entire family redefines the word "care." They truly care for their animals, they care for each other, and they put care into their lives. They genuinely care and value life as the precious gift it is. They are present with each moment, each life, and the many complications, beauties, and responsibilities contained therein.*
>
> *It's calving season, so all the pregnant heifers are about to give birth. Two of them have already successfully had their calves—thank goodness the weather has started to warm up. Emotions flood the air as everyone knows there are so many potentials for errors, mishaps, and unfortunate events; however, the excitement of birth and life seem to cloak looming tension and fear lingering about. Winter has almost come to its end, and spring is just around the bend. Another season to get up before the sun again.*
>
> *Communication occurs on almost a minute-to-minute basis. Progress, duties, projections, and tasks at hand are discussed.... Just like a true business platform.*
>
> *We are anxiously waiting in anticipation for a first-time heifer that is giving birth. Two hooves are already out of the womb, and the mother is groaning as she attempts to push her calf out. Annie is lovingly standing by just as a midwife*

assists a mother during an at-home birth. She is mostly concerned with ensuring the new mom doesn't give up. Annie stands just a few feet from another first-time mom with her own newly born calf. Although this may seem to be comforting to the heifer giving birth, it also serves as a distraction, which could lead to complications. Annie decides to intervene and drive the two away from the delivering heifer. She walks slowly, using caution, and speaks in loving, quiet tones as she approaches. Daisy, Annie's dog, and I are asked to stay back a few hundred yards so we don't add any stress to the situation. I have binoculars so I can watch the progress. The air is cold, but the sun is warm. The ground is muddy and nearly frozen as the sunshine aims to melt its hard surface, which also plays a dissatisfying role in the morning's efforts of work.

What a morning it turned out to be. Nothing can be assumed. I suppose that is a common misconception we involve ourselves in as humans: assumption. We assumed that the calf would be born on its own, we assumed the other pair were mother and child, and we assumed that we were just keeping an eye on natures course. All of these proved to be untrue. After Annie's many years of experience working in the fields told her that enough time had passed, she hesitatingly made the decision to assist in the delivery of the calf. She explained the various reasons why she did not want to intervene; the first being it will cause stress to the newborn, the second being the physical and emotional difficulty of the matter as well as the uncommon trauma it would inflict on the heifer, which may lead to abandonment of the calf. A few other fears Annie explained during this time included stillbirth, self-doubt, complications to the mother, and incompleteness of delivery. Keep in mind, although Annie is very strong for her size, she stands at about five foot seven and weighs no more than 130 pounds. She pales in comparison, a mere tenth, to the 1,300-pound pregnant heifer.

She faced many challenges after deciding to step in to help. I watched from a good hundred yards or so, waiting in anticipation for Annie to call me over with the backpack of emergency supplies. I followed her orders and kept my distance, but it was too late for the calf. After many attempts to revive him, his fate was sealed.

This experience was emotional. It was the first stillbirth I'd ever seen, or even been close to, really. It left me with just a hint more of understanding of what it means to be a farmer. I was in awe of these people. My interests were constantly captured by this family. I felt like a sponge soaking up all the newness around me. I couldn't help but to keep reaching, keep pondering, keep experiencing, and keep seeking the answers to my yet-to-be-determined questions. Now, I felt like a teeny tiny fish in a huge pond.

Process

I wouldn't necessarily say I was obsessed with the idea of killing things, but some people might have said that about me. I'd say that I am just a curious person, and I like to be involved in and execute actions that might fulfill my curiosities. In any case, death hasn't always fascinated me; it's life I have a great fascination for actually. But I have certainly had some goals on my bucket list to kill things and to do it myself. Only animals, of course, and solely for the mere purpose of understanding the process of harvesting meat for consumption. Once Annie caught wind of this, she made some arrangements for me to be part of some slaughters. Now, that's a good friend.

The first quadruped slaughter I partook in was with some colleagues of Annie's who were killing some of their own hogs—two to be exact. She let them know I was interested in learning how to harvest different animals. I had met a few of them briefly before, and they knew the gist of my story and my eagerness to learn, so I was welcomed to join, observe, and participate as much as I wanted.

The drive to the property where Annie would be leaving me for the evening was simply gorgeous. I drove myself in my truck, but I followed her in her truck through the winding countryside road that delved deeper into the rolling foothills of the Appalachian Mountains. We passed by amber waves of grain and various fields filled with lively herds of cattle and sheep. The anticipation for what was to come, along with the peaceful views of the area, orchestrated a harmony within my being that provided affirmation for my existence at that very moment.

For this endeavor, there were three men involved. One of the guys, Bradley, was a sixteen-year-old, hardworking towhead and had incredibly high energy and enthusiasm. He was also quite knowledgeable. I stayed by his side when I first arrived since I initially felt most comfortable with him, having already worked with him on the Reynolds' farm. It didn't take me too long to find common ground and settle in, so shortly thereafter, I was asking all three of the guys numerous questions and volunteering my idle hands.

"What can I do?" I asked with bloodthirsty eyes.

"First thing we'r' gon' do is shoot them suckers in the head," Bradley explained. "We just use this here .22 and aim right between the eyes. As soon as they drop, we stick 'em."

Frankly, I had no idea what "stick 'em" meant. I nodded my head as I watched in awe, and the adrenaline grew within me as I realized these guys do this often. How had I never been exposed to this before? I knew I was in for a real treat.

On the property where we were performing the slaughter, there was a setup that supported this regular process. On a concrete slab stood a hoist where they could lift the carcass in order to remove the hide and the entrails. Behind the hoist, there was a walk-in cooler that could hold about four carcasses. There were hooks dangling from the ceiling that were attached to rails, which made it easy to maneuver the two-hundred-pound, dressed animals. To the left of the freezer stood a commercial-grade shed filled with two large stainless steel sinks and various appliances that could cut, grind, slice, and seal a variety of meat.

About ten yards south of the processing setup, there stood a huge custom-made smoker. This smoker, they explained, could smoke an entire hog with the skin and head on. The smoker was made up of two steel drums welded together end to end and cut in half lengthwise in order to fit an entire hog inside. On occasion, they would prepare feasts for friends or family from homegrown, home-processed meat. This type of setup is exactly what piqued my interest.

"Stand back!" one of the guys hollered.

Pop! was the sound the little rifle made when the young man shot the first hog. The beast dropped instantly. The second guy quickly stuck it right in the jugular with a six-inch filet knife. Soon after, blood came pouring out of its neck. Just as you've seen in cartoons, the hog's tongue came flopping out of its mouth, and after a few twitches of its nerves, it settled into stillness. The hog was in the back of a livestock trailer, and it wasn't but seconds after this ordeal occurred that a river of bright red liquid began to flow from the opened door of the trailer and run along the dirt path as it naturally forged its way downhill. I was enthralled.

After letting the animal bleed out in the trailer for a few minutes, one of the guys brought over a tractor in order to haul the hog over to the hoist. These men proved their strength when the three of them got the carcass up into the tractor bucket. Once it was near the hoist, they put two hooks just under the each of the Achilles tendons and used the mechanics of the device to slowly raise it up in order for us to begin the actual breakdown of the beast. Once it was raised, they explained the importance of keeping the area cleaned with fresh water from the hose. They were constantly rinsing off dirt, debris, and blood from the animal and the surrounding area and equipment. The three of them worked in sync as they playfully joked and teased each other.

The oldest of the bunch, Bob, was the father of Bradley. It was his property where we were working that day. Bob was the leader of this operation, and it was quite clear that he was very experienced with the breakdown of animals. He would stress the importance of many little details of the process. He was well respected by both Bradley and his friend and sometimes colleague, Dale.

I knew Dale from my previous visits to Ohio, as he was a close friend of Annie's and the Reynolds family. I didn't know he would be at Bob's house that day, so when he pulled up to help with the slaughter, it completely changed my experience for the better. Dale had a friendly spirit and was not too bad on the eyes either. Naturally, I wanted to show my fervor for the endeavor and that I was not afraid to dive in and get dirty. Who knew that flirting while cutting up a carcass was a thing?

The first order of business, once the hog was hung, was to take off the hide. The animal hung from its hind legs with its head hanging near the ground. The process began by strategically using a very sharp knife to peel the skin away from the fat and muscle tissue. Cutting off the feet and head are a part of this process as well. At first, I just observed, but it wasn't long before the boys had teased me enough to make me grab a knife and dive right in.

The pig was warm to the touch, and the cold water from the hose caused steam to rise as it came in contact with the slimy fat of this freshly killed animal, which would soon be sizzling bacon. I noticed the care and precision each of the men used while industriously cutting around tendons and arteries. This same skill and caution, I would later find out, was used by most folks who worked in the business. This careful cutting not only prevents unnecessary mess and cleanup, but it also creates a beautiful dance between knife and subject, hence the reference of butchery as an art.

"She's almost twice as big as the last one we done," Bradley commented.

"Oh, really? Is this a common size for a pig to be butchered?" I asked inquisitively.

"Aw, no, ma'am! Haha!" He laughed. "This one here's a biggun!"

When Bradley finished getting the skin off of the head, he held the pelt up to his face, showing the perfect mask-like product he made, eye-holes and all. He joked that it could be a Halloween costume. This is a perfect example of the twisted sense of humor butcher's share, which I'm sure could relate to other's who have slightly off-the-grid occupations. Luckily for me, my sense of humor fit right in. I mean, you can't honestly tell me there isn't anything funny about blood, guts, and pig masks.

"What are ya'll gonna do with the head?" I asked.

"Meh, we'll probably just bury it somewhere in the woods. It's got a bullet in it, so some of the meat's no good."

"Could I take it home?" I asked, hoping to dive into some experiments in the kitchen with jowl meat and headcheese.

"I don't see why not." They laughed.

"Here, why don't you pose with your new buddy?" Dale held up the pig's head for me to get a picture with. I made the gesture that I was giving it a kiss—after all, its tongue was still sticking out. We all had a good laugh about that and continued to work.

In what seemed like one fell swoop, Dale removed the entrails of the beast. He explained the importance of not nicking any of the intestines with the blade due to the horrendous odor that would excrete if it happened. He meticulously cut around the anus of the animal and kept it intact with the colon, which led to the small intestine, large intestine, stomach, esophagus, and all the way up to the throat. It was pretty impressive to watch. It also opened my eyes to the reality and similarities of the human digestive system.

They had a large barrel with wheels on it that caught all of the innards. One by one, Bob explained the organs to me—the liver, the lungs, the heart, and so on. He said sometimes they keep some of these parts for consumption and sometimes they just toss them; it just depended on how much his wife wanted to use. More often than not, they had more leftovers than what they could eat, so much of it would get left for the vultures.

After the animal was skinned and the entrails were emptied, the men used a huge saw to cut down the length of the spine of the pig so it could hang in two identical but mirrored halves. By cutting it in half, it was easier to maneuver from the hoist to the rails in the cooler; there, it would hang, at least overnight, in order for the meat to cool and be prepared for processing. Once this process was complete, we hosed everything down well and repeated the steps with the second hog. This time, I helped a little more vehemently, and the boys guided me through removing the guts too. They also let me take the second head home. I couldn't have dreamed up a more perfect experience to satiate my curiosities and use my skills.

Once back at the farm, Cindy and I ended up working together to extract meat from the two heads. I'll never forget the look on Bruce's face when he walked into their house while Cindy and I were standing there with mallets, hand saws, and knives spread about the countertop. She stood with her hands held firmly on the skull of the pig while I had a large saw in my hands, trying vigorously to separate the skull bone into two halves. It turned out to be quite the endeavor. We feasted for days on that meat.

This was the second actual meat-processing slaughter I was involved in, thanks again to Annie. The first occurred about two months prior when Annie's friend Sean, who took me on my first hunt after the harvest party, needed some of his chickens to be processed, and he invited us over to help. He surely knew the right women to call for the job!

The night we harvested his chickens was a doozy. Sean showed us how to handle the chickens, and soon, we were slicing throats, hanging the birds to empty their blood, and removing their organs—or, as he put it, "reaching in and getting all fierce with it." Next, we dipped the chicken carcasses into a big pot of boiling water in order to open the follicles that held the feathers so we could easily pluck the birds. After the initial plucking, we took them inside to do a more meticulous job and to butcher some of the birds into halves, wings, and breast meat, depending on how he wanted to divide it up.

Sean's parents helped with the process, and all in all, it took the five of us about four hours to kill, process, and clean up about eight birds, though his parents actually only helped with the end of the process. We also made sure to take plenty of beer and bonding breaks throughout. Comradery, I've learned, is an important step in butchering, and I wasn't about to be a fun-crusher, even if I was eager to practice my bird slaughtering skills.

The third time Annie exposed me to slaughtering would become a game changer for me. In mid-September, just over six months after I moved to Ohio, Annie took me to one of the slaughterhouses where they sold some of their cows. Now, this was a legit, commercial setup for killing and processing animals. It was much bigger than the backyard setup I had experienced months before, although it was similar as far as the lineup for procedure and equipment.

This particular slaughterhouse, Lee's, would come to be my employer and would also house some rather dramatic changes for me. Luckily and thankfully, I established a relationship with the owner, George Butler, just weeks before the unraveling events that would influence me to shift my focus from learning the farm-life to following a lead into the meat-processing world. It's funny how life can present you with an opportunity or an "answer" before you even realize there is a question.

Alma

You've asked me to lie.
You've asked me to steal.
You've asked me to hurt,
and go against my will.

I'm part of the pain.
I'm a part of deceit.
I've been roped into the game,
and I want to retreat.

My compassion for others,
And need for what's right,
Lead me to ask,
How do you sleep at night?

Oh wait, I know—wrapped in the arms
Of illusion and despair.
You're feeding this beast,
And not looking into the mirror.

Have you ever been caught up in a situation and suddenly realized you needed to get out? Have you ever looked around and felt if you didn't leave at that very moment, perhaps you would cause something terrible to happen that you may possibly regret for the rest of your life? But were you willing to stay anyway? Have you ever come to a point where your moral compass pointed to the darkest of directions?

Within a few weeks of moving to Ohio, I was asked if I would be interested in helping with a cultural exchange project. And as we've established, at this point in my life, I was saying yes to any and all ideas that enticed the newness. This collaborative was one of many that exponentially expanded my world, but it wouldn't be until much later that I would realize just exactly what I signed up for.

This particular project involved bringing a group of Peruvian street performers to the Ohio Valley in order to do a tour of performances and workshops that would teach students about the contrasting culture of Lima, Peru, which was much different than that of Lima, Ohio, as well as expose various forms of Peruvian art. The work involved accumulating travel documents, scheduling performances and workshops with local schools and campuses, managing schedules, and coordinating rides, hotel stays, and meals for the group; most importantly, the goal was to create an incredible cultural experience for everybody involved.

When Annie's mother, Cindy, asked me to join her in bringing this endeavor to life, I was elated. The opportunity not only enticed me, but it seemingly swallowed me whole. I was enthusiastic about having a challenge and working on something I had never done before, and I was also excited to partner up with Cindy, as I'd grown to admire her as an intuitive, wise woman. Right away, she explained to me her vision, and we got to brainstorming.

Alma was the name of the performing arts group from Lima, Peru. They were mainly street artists who performed educational theatre with disciplines such as dancing, singing, acting, and the playing of a variety of musical instruments. Their focus was enlightening their audience about the dynamics and tribulations that can come as a result of living on the streets in a city with over nine million inhabitants. The group consisted of ten performers, ranging in age from eighteen to forty-five, who each had many talented and choreographed acts. The director, Mateo, had been performing and teaching workshops for decades, and his passion for the arts was evident in everything he did, from having a mere conversation with him to watching the breathtaking soliloquies of his performances. The group played a diversity of their native wind and percussion instruments, such as the cajón (pronounced cuh-hone), which is like a box drum that is usually sat upon while played by the musician, and the charango, which is a small Andean stringed instrument similar to a banjo with ten strings.

Alma was invited to come from Peru to Central Ohio to bring awareness, education, and entertainment for a two-week period. Cindy was moved and inspired when she was traveling abroad in Peru and witnessed the passion and talent of this particular group. Due to Cindy's fortunate circumstances, she was the head of the board for a trust in Ohio that had funds specifically for diversifying education and cultural exchange. The brilliant idea came to her to use her foundation's resources in order to bring this group to America.

The rural parts of the Ohio Valley are mostly made up of those from a Caucasian heritage. There are definitely some other ethnicities thrown into the mix, but some areas are predominately "Whiteville, USA." However, the community was hungry for culture, so the Ohioans involved were excited to welcome something new and different. The idea of bringing a group of foreigners to elementary schools, middle schools, high schools, and colleges around the area to teach workshops and expose children to the culture and performing arts of Peru was highly embraced among multiple communities and universities. After receiving confirmation from the various participating schools and businesses, Cindy moved forward with getting passports, funds, and details in order to make this vision a reality.

Once Alma landed in Ohio, my job was essentially to be the "den mother." I had to make sure they were fed and that they arrived at their respective workshops, housing locations, and performances in a timely manner. They needed three meals a day for thirteen people (the other three people included Mateo's significant other, his father, and Alma's photographer). Being the den mother to an all-male group was certainly going to be interesting, but I was up for the task.

Prior to their arrival, we rented a fifteen-passenger van and booked houses, hotel rooms, and other accommodations in the surrounding areas. We planned meals and made a relatively tight budget for the duration of their stay. We planned to grocery shop so we could make home-cooked meals for the group, but we also included takeout or dining out in our budget, which ended up being fun for some Elm Tree Pub patrons who were able to catch a free performance one night.

Thankfully, the Peruvian culture is familiar with dining as a large group, so when we prepared the meals, all hands were on deck. One day, a few of the guys were excited to cook their country's traditional food, so we took them to the market to buy ingredients and watched with adoration as they lovingly destroyed the farm's kitchen in the process of preparing some of their native dishes including rice,
anticucho, and causa.

"What the hell is going on up here?" I looked at Annie and laughed as I walked into the kitchen to see four of the guys around the kitchen island. One was stirring a large pot containing an unfamiliar dish, another was passionately chopping white onions in disarray on a cutting board, and the other two, with their backs to me, were each working on their own calamitous fares.

"Oh, just watching these professionals at work," Annie replied with hilarity as if she were watching children prepare food in the kitchen.

A quick glance out of the window revealed a few of the guys venturing around the farm. One was attempting to collect debris from the pool, two were goofing around on the tennis court, and one guy was admiring the horses in the barn. The man in the barn, Lucas, loved the horses so much he was cleaning the stalls merely to be helpful and give the horses a clean place to stand. I decided to go outside to enjoy life with our new friends.

By nature of my role with the group, I became well acquainted with everyone. I spoke and understood a little bit of Spanish, and some of them spoke a little English as well, so we were able to have conversations—relatively. A few of them embraced the fact that I didn't know a lot of Spanish, so there were times that I was unknowingly the butt of some jokes. All in good fun I was assured. But for the most part, our conversations were unique and meaningful.

"We all come from the same rock," Sofia, Mateo's girlfriend, explained, expressing to me the belief that, at one point, we are all formed from one initial element.

Throughout my time with the Peruvians, I would have opportunities to create bonds and have intimate conversations with each of them. Sometimes these bonds were made during the commutes with whomever would sit up front, and other times, it was during rehearsals or mealtimes. The exposure of one-on-one time with each of these beautiful souls enriched my life to a great extent. The Peruvian culture is one filled with passion, connection, and joy. I personally value these traits in my life and

123

relationships, so it made for the perfect common ground with my newfound comrades.

During this time, I still worked at the pub and I also worked part-time at the steakhouse in Columbus, so I had to juggle my schedule a bit in order to be helpful to the Peruvian escapades as much as possible. I did not sleep much during these two weeks. Some days, I would wake up and drive over an hour just to pick them up, get them breakfast, and then drive to another destination, all before 9:00 a.m. This was all part of the prearranged schedule Cindy and I worked out when we meticulously went over as many details as we could to coordinate their stay.

During their two-week stint, there was only one night off planned for these artists. Other than that, their schedules were jam-packed with workshops, performances, rehearsals, meet-and-greets, commutes, and other to-dos. Their night off was a Friday, and on that particular night, the guys had specifically stressed that they wanted to enjoy a night out in the city and go to a Hispanic dance club. Cindy and I kept this in mind when we arranged for housing and schedule accommodations. I agreed to take them out dancing and to be the designated driver.

Since I worked that evening, Cindy took them to dinner in the city, and I agreed to meet up after work in order to head to the nightclub. It was probably 11:00 p.m. by the time I arrived at the hotel and rounded up whomever wanted to hit the nightclub scene. I was exhausted, but I understood how excited these guys were to have a night off, so I was willing and ready to contribute to the experience. I'd say only about six of them decided to go out that night—the younger six of the bunch. It was a reasonably sized crew to keep tabs on, but by the time we got to the dance club, there was not much time left to enjoy the music. The club informed us they were announcing last call and would be closing soon.

We enjoyed the first nightclub for as long as we could, and then we followed some locals to another dance club that gave us basically the same news. Plus, we were told we had to pay some ridiculous cover charge at 1:00 a.m., so at this point, it was more annoying than enjoyable—at least for me. (Granted, I had been up early in order to get the group to their respective workshop, and then I had worked a full double shift at the restaurant. Then, I had to drive back to the hotel to round up the already semi-intoxicated bunch to take to the first club, and then to another club… You could imagine my agitation.)

When all was said and done, I was exhausted. The guys were tired too, and though the clubs hadn't quite gone as planned, they seemed fulfilled enough by the alcohol and efforts. Luckily for them, there was not much to do the next day except move to a new hotel and enjoy an evening hosted by a local Peruvian family. Unfortunately for me, I had to work another double shift that Saturday. Cindy had explained to me that she got me a hotel room in Columbus so when I dropped the guys off after clubbing, I could just stay there and then head to work the next morning. She would take over management duties for Saturday and Sunday morning, and we planned to meet the following Sunday afternoon.

I should note that I'm leaving out some details about fending off some of these young men. It wasn't all schedules and chauffeuring and meals. Although they were incredibly respectful and kindhearted, since the very first moment I met the group, flirtatious behavior and sexual advances were part of the gig. It was mostly in good fun, and if I'm being honest, there was one time where I actually kissed one of the guys, Samuel, in a moment of passion and weakness a few days prior at the farm. So I can understand why, after clubbing, he had made references about coming into my hotel room that night.

Although the kiss a few days before was enjoyable, I meant it when I said I was utterly exhausted. All I wanted at that point was to take a hot shower and get as much sleep as I possibly could before having another full day of work the next morning. By the time we actually made it back to the hotel that night, it was about 3:30 a.m. It had almost been twenty-four hours that I'd been awake, and I had been busy. All. Day. There was no way I wanted any sort of company. I wanted sleep.

With all that being said, now is the time I must shine a little more light on the situation, and to do that, I need to back up my story a little.

The day the Peruvians arrived, Cindy and I were ecstatic. She was mostly the mastermind behind the whole plan, but my detail-oriented mind helped to make this dream a reality. Alma was excited to come to America, some of them for the first time, and they were hoping to spread their love and beliefs internationally through their art. We were all high in anticipation and expectation for the weeks to come. This sort of experience had been the first for me as far as orchestrating and organizing a group, but my role definitely played to my strengths.

Cindy and I left the farm and drove together to pick up the rental van. The plan was that I would then drive the van from the airport about two hours away to the first destination where the group would stay and begin their tour of workshops and performances. Cindy would follow in her car, and we would coordinate the back and forth trips of car swapping and navigating how to get the group around for the next two weeks. Like I said, I was thrilled, practically chomping at the bit to meet this group and execute my duties.

But on the way to pick up the rental van, Cindy dropped a bomb on me. She admitted to me that one of the men in the group was her boyfriend. Cindy, Annie's *mother* and Bruce's *wife*, informed me that she was having an affair and that we were about to pick up her Latin lover from the airport. She told me she had been with him for six years and that they were deeply in love.

I was in shock.

I remember feeling torn and confused and certainly caught off guard.

What the fuck?! Really? What?!

These were certainly all thoughts I had in those brief moments when she explained the situation to me. As sickening as it is for me to now admit the truth, it took days for this information to really sink in.

"He's my soulmate," she explained.

"Like, how did you even meet?" I asked.

She explained to me that they met while she was traveling abroad years ago, and at first, it was just playful and innocent. But with connection and conversation, their relationship grew and expanded into fondness and eventually... love. The two stayed in touch for years and met each other around the world to forge, what she called, a beautiful bond where they both truly believed they were each other's soulmates.

"My mom had an affair on my dad, and eventually, she explained to me some realities about true love, so I get it," I excused the situation passively.

Although this was not untrue, I remember hating my own mother at the time and not understanding some realities of adulthood, relationships, and love. I later came to peace with her about her choices in life that were driven purely out of love, although in that situation, the love was not for my father and the cost was pricey. And once I became a young woman and had my own experiences with love, I eventually forgave my mother. So, at that moment in time, in the car with Cindy, I was able to excuse her so that I could stay focused on our mission ahead, but something still churned in my stomach.

Minutes after receiving this news, we pulled up to the airport. Cindy excitedly ran up to her boyfriend and threw her arms around him, and they showed each other great affection, completely oblivious to the world around them. This behavior, however, could have possibly been excused as the incredibly physical and affectionate nature of the Peruvian culture, where big hugs and kisses on the cheeks and lips were not uncommon upon greeting one another, which is a fact I would come to learn more in the coming weeks. But after Cindy let me in on her secret, I knew better.

Their zest for life was addicting, I'll admit. These people were so filled with love, life, energy, passion, and enthusiasm that I could not help but become completely engulfed in the present moments with them, allowing me to be unburdened for a brief moment. I was fascinated with the experience in which I was involved—it was quite magical after all. And I knew Alma was thrilled too. For some of these guys, it was like a dream come true to come to America to share their passions and talents.

In the van, on the drive to the cabin where they would stay the first two nights, the guys were all singing and one of the guys played one of the smaller stringed instruments. Their voices, laughter, and sweat filled the small space of the van and created a cocoon for their spirits. This intensity set the tone for the evening.

Once we all spilled out of the van, we dispersed as everyone got acquainted with this huge cabin tucked away in the woods and took a moment to welcome the now settling high of arriving to America. I was riding the high of the energy they exuded; my empathetic heart and spirit soared during the first hours of day one, although deep down, a small seed of desecration had been planted within me.

This disgusting seed was watered sporadically at first when I would witness the small hints of the affair. I tried my best to ignore the heaviness of this dark secret those first few days, thinking it was no big deal, that I could handle knowing this. And there was so much to distract me with all these incredible souls around that it was almost easy to shove it to the back of my mind. But secrets always have a way of surfacing.

After about a week, it became obvious to the group as well what was going on. There were a few days that the group stayed at two of the houses on the farms. We dined together, shared stories, made music, and experienced moments of laughter, entertainment, and conversation as the farm family and the Peruvians sat around tables and firepits, authentically enjoying each other's company.

I felt completely alone and utterly disgusted with myself for knowing all of the information I did. I had witnessed pure deceit when I saw Cindy's husband welcome her lover into his home and ask him genuinely inquisitive questions about his culture, passions, and career. This is when the knife began to turn in the now festering wound in my gut.

The next morning, a special conversation among Annie, her mother's lover, and myself would dump salt onto those oozing blisters and cause an agonizing separation of the genetically bonded atoms of my being. I could feel parts of myself being ripped to shreds in the deep moral fibers of my existence. My stomach churned, and I actually began to fall physically ill.

This is not okay. None of this is okay.

It finally hit me. The last straw. I had kept my mouth shut for ten days. The night I arrived at the hotel room after the exhausting ordeal of trying to entertain these entertainers during our night on the town, I opened the door to what I thought would be my haven to rest and recuperate, but instead, I was met with repulsion.

The bed was in complete disarray. An empty liquor bottle was lying on its side on the dresser of the hotel room. Sandals, toothbrushes, and towels were strewn about the room, and there was not one area of comfort or peace for me in that disturbed room. This was not a room booked for me to get a good night's sleep. No, not even close. This was the lovers' sex den.

To make matters worse, on the other side of the door, two different men were trying to coax their intoxicated selves into what should have been *my* hotel room in their hopes to provide me the least desired company imaginable at that moment. I was in shock. And I was so tired. I was beyond disgusted, far past mad, angry, and hurt. I felt betrayed. *That narcissistic bitch.* This was abominable, repugnant. *That selfish whore.* I was done. And I needed sleep. Without even taking any items of clothing off, I literally curled up into the tiniest ball on top of the still disheveled comforter and fell into a horrible nightmare-infested sleep.

In the morning, I actually vomited disgust. It didn't have the texture of food or the consistency of stomach bile. It was pure, uncanny disbelief of abuse and surfeit abhorrence. My head hurt. My heart bled. My soul shrank as a wicked witch would when exposed to sunlight. I melted. I melted into a depression and confusion, and I finally turned outward to some people I trusted to seek refuge.

There was a brief conversation I had had with Bruce where he asked me about a trip to Tennessee that Cindy told him she would be accompanying me on. This was another fucking lie. And I am not a fucking liar, but I lied to Bruce as I briefly played the smoke screen for

Cindy, my partner whom I now loathed. She was using me beyond simple misdirection. She had straight up roped me in and was playing me like a pawn in her attempt for checkmate in her selfish, thoughtless game. That was it. That night, I confronted her while driving together in her car back to the farm.

"You have to tell Bruce. I cannot live like this," I pleaded with her. It was difficult to confront her in her state of ecstasy.

"I won't tell him and neither will you," she retorted as if she knew she had some power over me and my actions.

"Cindy, I can't live like this. You are going to force me to move off the farm because I can't lie to your family."

Her response was blunt and harsh and basically the equivalent of "Okay, bye." I was in disbelief. I couldn't stand it. I couldn't stand her.

"I'm out. I'm not helping you with your stupid charade anymore. You can finish this project by yourself." I was so pissed I considered crashing the car in a moment of rage, or at least threatening to do it, but I held it together.

So many of my illness-centered thoughts were lost in those dark days of agony and turmoil. I couldn't believe how selfish she was and how she had played me, poisoned me with her infidelity.

Two days later, when I was out for a run, I called my brother back in Nevada. I explained everything to him with tear-filled eyes, choking on my words from emotion.

"Just tell Annie," he said in his monotonous voice.

That was it. That is what I could do.

I had wanted to tell Bruce the night before. I knew Cindy would not be home as she was up at a performance in Kenton, about forty-five minutes away. I had made up my mind to have a drink with Bruce at his house, as we had done many times before, and I would explain to him Cindy's affair, my unwilling involvement, and the utter heartbreak and disgust I felt for the entire situation. I had no idea how it would go, but that was the only thing I could make up my mind to do in order to get my conscience right. I would simply tell him. I had spent an entire day building up the courage to make that phone call, which I had done at about 9:00 p.m. that evening.

"Hey, Bruce. It's Karissa."

"Oh, hi, Karissa. How are you?"

"I'm doing alright, Bruce. Um, I was hoping to come over and have a glass of whiskey if you are up for it."

It had become a common and mutual enjoyment of Bruce's and mine to enjoy some whiskey and shoot the shit at his house after a long day's work. He knew I had been incredibly busy with the Peruvian escapades, and it was time for the harvest on the farm, so it was a busy time for him as well, which made for the perfect kind of evening to warm our spirits with spirits.

"Okay, that sounds great, Karissa. I have a long day tomorrow, so let's not make it a late one."

"Perfect. I'll see you in about ten minutes."

I had gotten in my truck, turned off the radio, and turned the engine over. I remember looking up to the sky and saying exactly this, "Okay, God, if you don't want me to do this. Then stop me." I had kept the music off as I drove down the dark driveway and headed up the rolling hill that would take me to the left turn onto Bruce's street. Only about five minutes from there would I arrive to his lane and make the half mile trip down the dirt road to his home—a drive I had done many times before.

It wasn't but three minutes into my drive that my phone had rang. "Hey, Karissa."

"Hey, Bruce. What's up?"

"Well, ya know, I am just so exhausted I was hoping we could take a raincheck on tonight."

"Oh, okay. Well, if you want. I am almost there though. I won't stay long," I had insisted.

"Really, Karissa, I am just dog-tired. I could pass out this very minute."

"Okay then, Bruce. We can shoot for another night. I totally understand."

"Great. Thanks."

"No problem. Get some rest."

"You too, Karissa. Bye."

I was relieved. I pulled over and cried. I bawled. I cried so hysterically and thankfully that I just sat there in silence and darkness on the side of the road for about twenty minutes. "Thank you," I whispered, knowing the divine intervention was the only way I would be stopped from doing something I knew I would most certainly regret.

On one hand, it was none of my business; however, on the other hand, I was forcibly put in the middle of this sticky situation, which in turn made it my business. It was my character and my integrity that were brutally tested and beaten throughout this time as I was called to lie to and mistreat those I loved and who loved me too. They had provided for me for the past year. Annie had taken me in to live in her home, and we had become like sisters; Bruce had welcomed me into his business and life, paying me for my contributions on the farm and gifting me with his experience, wisdom, and friendship. And I was now in a situation where I had lied to their faces and clearly abused the beautiful bonds formed over the past year. I was defeated. I went back to my basement quarters, and I rested with some peace that I did as much as the universe had allowed me to before stopping me in my tracks.

The next day, after speaking to my brother, I knew, and somewhat dreaded, that it was Annie who I should tell. She was my friend, and oddly enough, it had been a friend of mine who, when I was just twelve years old, had told me about the affair my mother was having. So there was a tiny part of me that understood just exactly how Annie might feel. I allowed that inner Karissa to recall the surprising safety and comfort that came from hearing such devastating news from a friend. I made my mind up: As soon as I saw Annie, I would tell her.

It just so happened that when I returned from my run, Annie was out cleaning the stalls in the barn. I walked straight out to the barn and announced, "Annie, I have to move."

Something about my tone must have implied my seriousness, as her and I frequented jokes of all ranges and dialects, and she knew this was no joke. She looked at me directly in the eyes and said, "Oh yeah, KJB? Why's that?" She kept raking the straw in the stall and lifting it into the wheelbarrow next to her.

"Because your mom is having an affair on your dad." I choked as I barely let the words fall from my lips.

Her bold, brown eyes were instantly tear-filled when she caught my gaze again. "Huh, well, I kinda figured that." She paused for a moment and then said, "So, what's it got to do with you?"

"It's with one of the Peruvians," I cried. "And I've had to lie to you and your dad to cover for her, and I can't do it anymore."

She stopped what she was doing for a moment, and it was obvious she had questions, but she also had work to do. So, she forged on in her tasks, and we separated for a few hours before reconvening with some wine to talk a little further.

I hate to admit that I felt instant relief, as if I had just gone to the bathroom after holding it in for days. It was out of me. The words. The truth. The lies. They were out of me. What would come next though, I had no clue.

I decided to take my dogs and get the heck out of dodge for a few days. I went to visit my mother in Tennessee, just a six-hour drive away. I already had a visit planned to go see her, so I just left a few days ahead of schedule. I figured it would be a safe place for me to hide out and recover. I could do no more, be it damage or good.

Reconciliation

I had backed away from my intricate involvement on the farm. I still lived with Annie and Olivia, but by the time the holiday season rolled around, I was now working part-time at the slaughterhouse and full-time at the steakhouse in Columbus. My roommates had nicknamed me "K-Busy," because I was always on the go, as per my energetic, industrious nature. I still slept in my basement quarters, but other than that, I didn't spend much time in Lima anymore. Once again, I fervently isolated myself from discomfort.

I liked keeping busy with all of my various forms of employment. Working at that steakhouse was high on the list of my most enjoyable time spent in Ohio. My coworkers solidified my understanding of the heart of America, each with their own passions, quirks, and personalities. Many of them had worked there for a number of years, and the dynamic of the restaurant set the stage for a bona fide entertaining environment. The in-house butcher, Fred, was probably the best character of all, always sharing stories about his various baby mamas, grandkids, and dangerous pit bulls. He'd worked there over a decade and knew all the ins and outs of steakhouse butchery. There was an in-house dry-aging room filled with primal cuts of beef, each with a rotation date pinned to it, and this is where Fred spent his days. He had a little area that housed a bandsaw and cutting board tables. I was elated when the managers granted me permission to work with Fred a few days a week to hone my newfound craft and learn from yet another talented butcher. He always brought in his own Pepsi, and he knew everybody's business. He was genuine and loving, and he loved to talk and tell stories. He'd sure been through a lot in his life, and he had the scars to prove it. He taught me the ways of his world and encouraged me that I was a natural. He joked that I needed to slow down a bit so I didn't wave any red flags that his job could be performed any quicker; he was paid by the hour after all, and he was the only butcher they had.

The steakhouse offered a reprieve for me, and friends like Fred helped to keep my mind off of the sticky situation in Lima, but even though I grew content in my new routine, I still faced great unsettling feelings. Though I knew how affairs could and might happen, I still couldn't sort through this mess. I had been through this before, but it somehow felt more complicated. I found myself clinging to Claire. She was someone who knew both Cindy and me well, and she was savvy to all that was going on in my world. She spent hours listening to me vent and ambivalently encouraging me to just worry about myself. She even invited me to stop by her house on my way to work Christmas morning so I could enjoy the holiday cheer and watch her kids open their gifts. I was met with an outpouring of love when I showed up at her house, and she had some fifteen presents with my name on them. Each, of course, was meticulously wrapped in different holiday wrapping paper. I opened my bounty with delight and was baffled with joy by a set of holiday pajamas she'd gotten me that matched the same outfits she'd gotten herself and her children. Family photo time! These gestures made me feel so welcomed, so merry and bright. If anything, it showed me that when trials and difficulties prevail, loved ones are the remedy.

One day, back in November, while adamantly confining myself in the Nevada Suite, I felt the ache and longing for my friendship with Cindy. Although she had royally pissed me off, I couldn't help but miss her powerful influence in my life. After all, we had a lot of fun together and she had helped me pursue any and all curiosities of my heart that I presented to her. We had often destroyed her kitchen with exciting, exotic adventures, such as butchering pig heads, making homemade pastas, and collaborating our efforts while hosting multiple gatherings at her house. Shit, we even successfully executed bringing a group of foreign strangers to America. Although that proved to be an overall predicament, it was technically a success. We hadn't spoken in a while, and by this time, the cat was out of the bag. She had her hands and heart full as she dealt with her own exposure of the truth, and I had been struggling myself trying to refit my pieces together after my perfect Ohio world was blown up. But the truth now was, after all was said and done, I missed her. I missed my friend.

I had attended her yoga classes pretty regularly up until our disquieting separation. So that evening, while sitting in my room, I called Claire to see what she thought about me going to one of Cindy's yoga classes as a gesture to break the ice. Over the phone, Claire encouraged me that it was not a bad idea, and she knew Cindy better than I, so I trusted her opinion; in fact, I was glad for it. I decided to show up unannounced to one of her regular classes. I quietly strolled into her studio a couple minutes after her class began. *Damnit, I'm always late.* The look on her face was all Cindy, compassionate and welcoming; however, I searched the air diligently for any lingering animosity. It wasn't there. I unfolded my mat and discreetly blended into the class.

I felt the same healing that evening that I'd felt time and time again from engaging in my practice with her as my guide. Cindy was, after all, a healer. Her gift to the universe derived from her connectedness to her own spirit and to those around her. After enduring all of the horrible pain from the two short months prior, I invited the celestial feelings of peace into my soul. We exchanged a few cordial sentiments before I left that evening, and although it still took another month for us to have an actual heartfelt conversation face to face, I knew this was the beginning of the healing process for both of us.

I received a phone call from Bruce late in November, not long after I made my first appearance at Cindy's studio. He invited me over for that glass of whisky that was long overdue. I was nervous and hesitant to acquiesce to his offer because I hadn't spoken with him at all since the night I had called him about six weeks prior. I wanted to go, not only to apologize and to explain my involvement, but also because I missed his influence in my life as well. We too had forged an unlikely friendship over the previous season, and he held a special place in my heart.

I had heard through the grapevine that Bruce and Cindy had been working on their situation. None of the details were my business, but I cared so deeply for every party involved. I was intricately woven into their story, not necessarily by my own hands. Each character had played respective roles in my story too. Annie was my friend and roommate and an idyllic figure in my mind. Cindy had been my partner in a whole roost of shenanigans and eye-opening experiences; I had grown to love her as a friend, mother, sister, and teacher. And then there was Bruce. The hard-working, honest-to-the-core, morally upright cowboy who lived the dream I once owned. I had built relationships with each of them that were irreplaceable, and it seemed, without much warning, the entire situation had crumbled before my eyes.

It was late when I arrived at Bruce's home that evening. He had a bottle of Laphroaig scotch on the large oak, dining room table with two glasses poured. He welcomed me into his home and returned to the seat at the head of the table where there was evidence he had been nestled prior to my arrival. Only two lights were on in the house, which created a somewhat melancholy atmosphere. The lines on his face were weathered, like the leather of his worn-in saddle. His eyes appeared tired and sad, yet his demeanor was amicable.

We talked for hours that night. He shared with me his accrued wisdom and recent pain like he had never done before—this time from a broken and vulnerable place.

"Karissa, I am just so sorry," he remarked. "This whole deal isn't quite what you signed up for, is it?"

"I'm sorry, Bruce." I tried to remain brave and hold it together. "I'm sorry for lying to you. I don't even know what to say or do anymore."

"Look, Karissa, you don't need to be sorry." He held a fatherly tone as he reassured me that it would all be okay. "I want to thank you for showing integrity and being honest. I can't imagine this has been easy for you."

"Bruce, I love you all so much. Your family has been so good to me, and I just feel…horrible."

"Well, you are kind of part of this family now, aren't you?" He chuckled, and we both acknowledged the inevitable truth that neither of us could escape. We shared a brief moment of joy and cheered our peaty drinks.

During the conversation that evening, Bruce painted me a picture with his words. He described the precious and powerful image of marriage in his mind. He explained how the sum is meant to be greater than its parts. He told me he had been married to Cindy for over thirty years and summarized the great struggles they'd overcome in the past. Although he was devastated from the situation, he said wouldn't trade a moment of their story.

His hurt seeped through his words as tears occasionally streamed from his eyes throughout our conversation. I'd never seen this side of Bruce. He contemplated regrets of working too much, not being emotionally available, and putting the farm's needs over his wife's. He admittedly embraced his roles as a man, a father, a farmer, and a husband that evening. He made his way through his feelings and memories into a place mingled with acceptance, defeat, solace, and steadfast certainty. Bruce knew the man he was, he knew the dreams he fostered, and he took full responsibility for his own role in their story.

The time, space, and spirits we shared that night brought our friendship to a deeper level. I felt a sense of calmness grow within me from these baby steps of respite from the situation. Although I still anguished over my circumstances, the internal pressure within me began to diminish. I could see the light at the end of the tunnel. I knew that confronting my unease would bring more healing than running away from the hurt, which I so often did in the past.

It was a few days before Christmas when I worked up the courage to once again make my way over to headquarters. With Annie's insight, I knew Cindy was home alone. I swallowed all of my apprehensions and made my way to her with a peace offering and hopes for reconciliation. The sun was out, and it was the most beautiful winter day I had witnessed so far in Ohio. There was no blaring frostbitten wind. No snow. Only sunshine and tranquility filled the air.

The roar of my diesel didn't allow for a subtle entrance onto her property, but it was probably for the best for her to know who was arriving. She met me on the porch as she respectively filled her dogs' bowls with their food.

"Hey, Kris," she greeted me with benevolence.

"Hi, Cindy Jo. I hope I'm not interrupting you," I coyly proceeded. My eyes were filled with sincerity as I searched for the courage to apologize. I studied her face and body language to measure the level of appropriateness of my being there.

"I was just about to take Bruno for a walk," she said. "Would you like to join us?"

"I'd love that."

"I'm just going to grab my shoes. I'll be right back," she turned to go inside. The screen door closed abruptly with a slam brought on from the tight spring. This echoed in my mind as I'd heard that same exact sound many times before.

I patiently waited on the porch while the dogs ate their food. I stared out over the pasture, watching the horses frolic with each other on the hillside. I breathed in the familiarity and serenity of the view. I had grown accustomed to this farm, fishing on the ponds, walking and horseback riding through the woods, helping in the gardens, but this time, I felt like an outlier simply observing the scenery. My gut toiled with unease as I anticipated the next moments.

As soon as Cindy came outside, I squared myself to face her with an open stance. "Cindy, I am so sorry. For everything." I began to well up with tears.

"Oh, Kris." She grabbed my hand. "It's okay." She comforted me with her motherly embrace. "I'm sorry too."

I could tell it wasn't easy for her either, but with her sixty-some years of wisdom and life experience, I felt the situation was genuine. We hugged. We cried. And we stood on the porch for a moment. Arm in arm, we then made our way toward the pond. We strolled in silence with the sun glaring upon us. After we passed the barns and the house fell out of our sight, the conversation grew, and we began to reminisce on the good times we shared and the exploits we conquered. We intimately expressed our frustrations, regrets, and love for each other and the entire situation. I knew her, and she knew me, and we both knew our story was far from over.

Juke

There's a saying, and it goes, "People come into your life for a reason, a season, or a lifetime."

But I believe some people can come into your life for all three.

I called him Juke because he loved music. He related everything in life to a song like Motown Mondays or Tuesday blues day. He would often hum his son's favorite movie theme songs, and he watched the Grammys like it was the presidential inauguration. Even after we ended our relationship, he would send me songs on YouTube as we grieved through the process of our breakup. To this day, I sporadically receive a joyful musical encouragement, a sweet new beat, or a classic oldie from my jukebox.

I met Juke at Smith and Wollensky. I'd worked there about six months before we ever really had an actual conversation, other than the brief banter between coworkers. And let's just say, he wasn't the friendliest guy at the place. Actually, he could have fallen under the category of disgruntled employee because he always seemed kind of angry, bitter, or upset over something. To be honest, after seeing his personality...um...shine, I steered clear of him. Although, there were times when we'd be both standing, waiting for the bartenders to give us our drink orders, and we would make small talk. Being the inquisitive extrovert that I am, I'd ask questions about his personal life and roots. I came to learn he had a son and a very humble perspective, despite what might easily be assumed of him.

One day in September 2015, Juke overheard me mentioning to another employee that I might be looking for somewhere to stay closer to work as we had a very busy week coming up and I commuted over an hour each way to the steakhouse from the farm. Our managers notified us that many of us would be working double-shifts for many days during Wine Week. Wine Week was an event hosted by our employer that offered the public a week-long wine-tasting featuring different types of highly rated wines. It was kind of a big deal, especially for the value. The idea was to get people in the door and have them learn the wines that we would be adding to the coming menu. As a new employee never having worked a Wine Week, I was both anxious and nervous for the event, but moreover, I dreaded the commute and lack of sleep I would have after working so many hours in one week. However, I was reassured that it would be lucrative and well worth my efforts—and we've already established how I feel about earning a few extra bucks.

I decided I should try to find a closer place to stay, but my four-legged friends were making it a little difficult to arrange since I didn't want to leave them on the farm. I needed somewhere to stay for maybe two to three days where I could bring my dogs with me. When Juke heard me say this to another coworker, he later approached me in the parking lot and informed me that he had a big house with a yard and that I was welcome to stay in one of his spare bedrooms. To be honest, at the time, I'd assumed he was married or had his baby mama at home because I knew he had a son, but I later came to find out he was a single father whose son had autism and lived with him full-time. After a few days of trying to find other options, and the pressure of Wine Week approaching, I asked Juke if I could really take him up on his offer. He welcomed me to come check out his house and see the extra room, so I did.

He was kind of a quiet guy outside of work. He was charming, polite, well-mannered, and well-spoken. He was full of jokes and laughs, and he was 100 percent non-judgmental. His house was actually clean and well-stocked with books, cooking supplies, and power-tools. (Those three are a dangerous combination for this girl.) I started to wonder if there was more than meets the eye with this guy. He showed me where I could sleep, where I could put the dogs, and where the bathroom was that I could use. I was impressed—not only with his home, but with him. He was so different than the grouchy guy I knew from work. That first evening he showed me his house was short and sweet, and it made me feel comfortable with the idea of bringing my dogs over for a little Columbus stay-cation.

To be honest, I didn't really think much of staying with Juke at first. His house was a place to stay with the internet and cable, which we didn't have out at the farm. Oh, and the endless supply of hot water, that was a glorious bonus! What a treat! These are things you might take for granted in our day and age, but farm life will teach you quickly to appreciate them.

The first night I stayed at his house, we sat on couches on opposites sides of the room from each other, watching the TV and having a conversation; we were just getting to know one another. We talked about our high school experiences, exchanged stories from our youth, and explained what our family lives were like. It wasn't at all like a date; we were just two coworkers getting better acquainted in a very comfortable environment. This conversation set the tone and connection for a beautiful friendship that would soon blossom into something more.

Over the course of the next couple weeks, I experienced some tension at the farm, so I began to pick up more hours at the steakhouse. Within about two months, Juke and I had become almost best friends. We

146

would talk often and had our inside jokes, and he would take me on little adventures around Columbus, to shows, parks, restaurants, and such. I guess we were dating, but I wouldn't allow myself to believe that at first. In my mind, he was just a friend who pursued my company quite earnestly. I do remember the first time I started to develop feels for him though. It was when he was in full-on "daddy-mode." What is it about men in daddy-mode that is so attractive to women?

One night, while sitting in my truck after our shift, we were enjoying some snacks I packed for my long commute.

"Would it be okay if I kissed you?" he asked while looking into my eyes.

"Okay." I smiled giddily.

I was grateful to have had the comfort, support, distraction, and companionship during the emotional dance I was experiencing after the intense situation on the farm. By now, everyone was well aware of the affair, so I steered clear of the family as much as possible. I still lived with Annie and our friendship was unscathed, but I knew she was hurting, so I did my best to just be a good friend and roommate.

With Juke, I could relax and have fun amidst the sadness and angst. I was hesitant to admit that I'd found a new fondness in him. He had struck my fancy, but I wasn't too sure how deep I'd been nicked. I was curious and attracted—that was for sure. In fact, he was the first journal-worthy boy in Ohio.

Looking back, Juke entered my life at the most opportune time. I needed refuge. I needed comfort and an outlet for the all-encompassing emotions that ran through my veins. I needed a friend. I lived so far away from my home and all that was familiar to me, and after learning about the affair, there was a period of time where I had basically estranged myself from those who came to be my family on the farm. But I also needed someone to care about me, who allowed me to be broken and vulnerable. I had felt so guilty and tormented for quite some time, and I had stuffed it all so deep within me that most everyone still only saw the happy, outgoing, friendly, fun Karissa.

Luckily for me, Juke was the kind of guy I could fully be myself with, and he gladly gave me both the freedom and support I needed. For a while, we complemented each other in regard to what we each were experiencing during that time in our lives.

In early 2016, we took a trip to Nevada so my friends and family back home could meet him. It was the first trip home I'd taken since I moved to Ohio the previous year, and it came at just the right time.

We were met with a delightful surprise when we noticed a public figure sitting just a few rows in front of us on the airplane. It was Temple Grandin, a woman who not only had autism, but was a spokesperson on the subject. Being a professor in animal science, she was also a consultant for the livestock industry as she'd studied animal behaviors her whole life. Once we realized she was sitting alone, I unbuckled my seatbelt and kindly asked her if we could speak with her for a few minutes. She obliged. Of course, I had a million questions I wanted to ask her about the livestock industry, but more importantly, Juke was so anxious to speak with her about raising his son. He spent about fifteen minutes being encouraged and affirmed that his fatherly efforts were most likely on point. This random occurrence set the sublime tone for the rest of our trip.

When we landed in Reno, the entire valley was covered in snow. I was so happy to be back home after enduring a difficult season back in Ohio. We spent a week doing touristy-type things around my neck of the woods, and I enjoyed showing Juke the treasures hidden in the glorious Sierra Nevada Mountains. We went skiing, we ate all-you-can-eat sushi, we spent an evening strolling the streets of Virginia City, and we even started the small project of renovating the master bathroom at my house. You know, typical vacation stuff. I was glad to be home for a short getaway, and I was thankful Juke was with me. This time solidified the fact that he was more than just a friend.

It wasn't long after that vacation that I finally agreed to be his girlfriend. We were rather transparent with each other, and I knew the winds of change were in the air for me. I was unsettled at the farm and now caught up in the whirls of romance. I knew it was time to leave SP, and I debated my next move heavily. *Should I get my own place? Should I stay put and endure the awkwardness? Should I leave Ohio?* Shortly thereafter, I moved in with Juke. It was an exciting reason to leave Annie's house and ease some of the residual tension from the previous months. Although it was bittersweet to leave the place that enticed me to move across the country, I was excited to start a life with Juke. Not to mention I had seemingly found a new reason to stay in Ohio.

We had a good, short run of it, but it turned out that the demands of being a single parent were far more than the level of commitment I could agree to. I originally had big plans for us, but after some time, I knew I just wasn't ready to settle into the responsibility of parenthood, co-parenthood, or really just dating someone who had a more important priority than the free-spirited life I embraced. This was a harsh truth I realized and swallowed. I felt guilty and sad, but my heart was convicted to run my race solo. So, within just a few months, we painfully decided to just be friends. Although he encouraged me that

I could stay at his house, I knew it wasn't right. Two short months after moving in, I moved out.

I debated where I should go, once again pondering the same questions I'd asked myself some sixty days prior. After some time, I was presented with the idea of moving into the place where it all began: the Reed farm, Annie's grandparent's home. Being eighty-eight and ninety-two had left Pop and Bee in need of a little extra physical support around the house, and for me, well, I was able to live rent-free on a farm with my dogs. They lived halfway between the slaughterhouse and the steakhouse where I worked, so it was perfect for me to commute to both jobs. And they welcomed me with open arms.

Although Juke and I had broken up romantically, we still remained close friends; this, I valued greatly. He helped me move out of his home and onto the Reeds' farm. He would come to visit and even volunteered to help with some of the manual labor they needed around their house whenever he could. More than we cared to build a life together as a couple, we both valued the genuine friendship we built and supported each other in the healthiest ways possible. As it turned out, Juke was my saving grace and guardian angel during multiple distressful endeavors.

I am so thankful for the decision to move in with the Reeds. I have always had a servant's heart, and it fulfilled me incredibly to feel so useful. Bee loved referring to me as her live-in chef, and I adored my role as the adopted granddaughter. Pop and I would do puzzles together, and when appropriate, he would politely ask if he could correct my English. Oh, how I love and appreciated that! The three of us would gather around their modest table in the den and watch *Antiques Roadshow* or some other "quite interesting program," as Bee would say. Even though she didn't drink much, Bee would always offer me a glass of wine with dinner as she oohed and aahed about the meals I made.

I experienced a magnificent time of both freedom and purpose. The dogs and I had acres and woods to roam at our disposal, and my little Tater Tot got to swim in the pond whenever her little doggy heart desired. We all got a kick out of hearing the faint yelp from her splashing around in the water at various times of the day. The pieces of my life were falling together quintessentially, and I felt truly at home. Living with those incredible people turned out to be one of the most joyous times in my life.

It wouldn't be long, however, before it also became one of the most trying times in my life. Within the next six months, I would experience catastrophic trauma that would turn my Midwestern odyssey upside down.

Become

      Initially, I found myself feeling rather lost as I settled in on the Reed farm. It was late spring of 2016. I no longer worked at the pub in Lima, I no longer dated my closest confidant, and I no longer lived or worked on the Reynolds' farm. Thankfully, it was only a few months after the dramatic reveal of the affair that I was able to rekindle my relationships with all parties involved. However, things didn't fit the way they had before. Everyone was still recovering from the backlash of this spilled secret, so I made sure to keep my schedule completely full to avoid the unpleasantness of the situation. This pattern of busyness and avoidance had proven to be a recurring theme in my life—though it would be years until I grasped this truth as an actual hindrance to my ability to cope with hardship. I've since learned you must face your fears and struggles head on in order to actually heal those festering wounds, but at the time, keeping busy and charging ahead was my way of moving forward.

      In the previous months, when I transitioned myself from the alluring country life to a more familiar city life when I temporarily moved in with Juke, I forged new friendships with coworkers and eagerly participated in all the local activities that called to my heart. Columbus was a fun city filled with an incredible array of delicious eateries, live music venues, and a contagious sense of community, so it was easy for me to acquaint myself with yet another new perspective. I felt fortunate and fulfilled amidst all of my wavering circumstances, even though uncertainty hovered above me with every move I made.

      It was around this time that my friend Jill graduated from grad school in Florida. She was moving back to Nevada that summer, and she asked me if I would take the journey with her. Of course, I didn't hesitate to return the favor and help her move across the country. With zero tension from all of my employers, I was able to take some time off. Since I was living rent-free on the Reed farm and I had just severed the ties to a brief romantic courtship, my circumstances were ideal to take a leave of absence. We orchestrated how we would coordinate this trip, since we wanted to make the most out of another trek through the States.

I drove to Tennessee so that I could leave my dogs and my truck with my mom for the time being. From there, I flew to Florida to really commence the mission. When I arrived, Jill picked me up at the airport and informed me that since she had to finish some last-minute projects with her work before her departure, she hadn't even begun to pack her apartment, even though she needed to be out of there in three days. *C'mon, Jill. Really?* The airport seems to be a common place for people to drop surprising news on me, but my love for this girl overpowered the annoying realization that I would spend the next two days packing her things, cleaning her appliances, and pestering her with questions like, "Do you want to keep this? Where does this go? Why the hell do you have this?" All the while, she tirelessly sat in front of her laptop, trying not to succumb to the pressure that was a result of her procrastination.

Did I mention she lived on the third floor? I can't tell you how many trips I took up and down the stairs, throwing bags of trash in the dumpster and precisely filling the U-Haul trailer with her things. Luckily for her, I was up for the task—not to mention I felt indebted to her for helping me move, and we know I can't let a favor sit unreturned. Besides, this is the kind of shit friends do for each other without hesitation, question, or judgment, right?

Even though it was a lot of work and a bit stressful, it was also quite comical, and we made the best of it as we got it all done.

Once she turned in the keys to her apartment, we started our drive to Orlando, where my cousin lived and offered to put us up for the night. We aimed to stay anywhere we could for free in order to reduce the cost of this feat. As a treat and a kick off to our trip, Jill's mother offered to pay for us to spend a day at Universal Studios Florida. Needless to say, we spent the entire time at the Wizarding World of Harry Potter. The prior few days had been arduous, so it was oh-so-fun to destress, drink Butterbeer, and let our enchantment play in the theme park that day.

From there, we made our way up to Tennessee to grab my dogs and crash with my mom—another cozy, brief, and complimentary bed and breakfast for the books. The next day just so happened to be July 3rd, so we arose early and headed west. One of us posted to social media that we were en route from Tennessee, and lo and behold, I received a text from none other than AMD, who invited us to a Fourth of July "blob" party in the heart of America. We didn't know exactly what it meant, but we knew we couldn't miss it.

The night we arrived, we had no idea what was in store. Apparently, a blob party involves one of those big, inflatable "blobs" that rests on a pond and is meant for someone with an adventurous spirit—obviously, I was all about it. Since I didn't bring my bathing suit to the party, I had to strip down to my skivvies in order to participate. I eagerly versed myself with the technique that would soon send me flying into the air. For the one being sent off, it all starts with an initial belly flop glide onto the blob. Once on the apparatus, you gotta carefully scooch out to the far end, making sure not to slide off into the water below.

When you're ready for launch, there is a ladder situated behind the blob that is to be climbed by the person who serves as the launching weight. The weight will ultimately send the rider into the air for a flying thrill that ends with a splash. Unbeknownst to me, as I sat with my back to the ladder, nervously anticipating the countdown that would let me know when liftoff would occur, not one but *two* people decided to send me flying.

"Three…two…one…" the group chanted behind me.

It was a dark summer night, and the glare of the bonfire and headlights from latecomers to the party were the only sources of light around. I soared into the night sky being forcibly twirled head over ass in midair. I must have flown over thirty feet high, and the smack of my body on the water stung like that of a blistering sunburn. I squabbled with the water for a moment, seeking a sufficient breath of air while trying to maintain my composure in front of the cheering onlookers. A friendly Midwesterner dove into the water to make sure I could swim out of the pond safely. The laughter and applaud from the crowd only enticed me to do it all again. Now that's the kind of party I'm looking for!

AMD, once again, cordially offered us a place to stay—this time, three dogs and two girls. And to our increased pleasure, aside from the blob party the previous night, his family also warmly welcomed us to join them in a holiday barbeque feast. We spent the next day lackadaisically enjoying Cornland, Illinois. As the dogs roamed the acreage of the farm, Jill and I rested and recuperated, preparing for the continuation of our journey the following day.

Our day off flew by, but it was just what we needed to motivate us to hit the road and hit it hard. The next day, we decided to get an early start and put as many miles behind us as we cruised through Iowa and Nebraska. We drove from six-thirty in the morning until eleven at night, only making a few pit stops along the way. We had made it to Kimball, Nebraska, when we decided to pull off and get some rest. It was late, we were all exhausted, and our selection of vacancies were few and far between.

After a good night's sleep, we checked out the map and realized how close we were to Colorado.

"How do you feel about taking a detour and checking out the Colorado Mountains?" I asked Jill as we lay on the hotel bed, watching whatever mystery crime show was on the television.

"Oh, I'm *so* down!" Jill replied with her agreeable attitude I love so much.

So, it was decided. We would mosey to Colorado for a camping excursion in the mountains. Thanks to Google Maps, we meandered through the dirt roads of the Arapaho and Roosevelt National Forest until we landed at a place called Red Feather Lakes. We were all packed into her Jeep with a U-Haul trailer in tow. Needless to say, we stuck out like a sore thumb in the wilderness that day, but we didn't care. We were just out to have fun, make memories, and enjoy the journey. Once we parked and settled in, we took the dogs to the lake to swim. We had plenty of food and were quite pleased with our makeshift campsite. We basked in the peace of having nothing to do and nowhere to be by any certain time.

Two uncomplicated days later, we found ourselves back in Nevada. Our first order of business was to get Jill unpacked and settled. Our second order of business: sushi. We both missed the all-you-can-eat option that seems to only be offered in the Silver State. We stuffed ourselves with practically everything on the menu, a partial reward for completing our trek and a mini celebration for what was to come. For Jill, it was time to find a job in her official field and rekindle her familiarity with the 7-7-5. And for me, it was time to unwind, enjoy being at my own house with my dogs, and in time, navigate my way back to Ohio.

I was blessed to have the entire summer off. Since I had rented out my room, I played the guest role in my own house and settled in on an air mattress in our third bedroom, which we had converted into a home gym. I made it my mission to move at a slower pace than I had during the previous year in Ohio. Even though I found myself in a transitionary state and my situation was now far different than when I originally set out to learn about farming, I felt like Ohio wasn't done with me yet. After all, I had yet to kill a deer from horseback with my bow. I couldn't move back to Nevada without at least attempting to cross that goal off of my bucket list, though from the comfort of my own home, the idea of pulling the plug on my Ohio adventure was tempting.

Not long after arriving to Nevada, I attended a Wanderlust Festival, which was a yoga festival filled with hippies and yogis alike. My friend Taylor and I were strolling through the main area of the event where vendors and performers congregated in order to attract the public and participants. A young couple was sitting on the ground with typewriters in front of them, writing personalized haikus for those passing by. They looked rather unkempt with their messy hair and tie-dye apparel, but they radiated joy and love. They invited us to sit and partake in their offerings—for free. So, we had some haikus written for us by these loving street artists.

At the time, I was pondering the idea of moving back to Nevada, but I hadn't felt it in my heart with a definite conviction. When the gentleman writing my poem asked me what I would like my poem to be about, I simply replied, "Home." While we waited for the couple to produce our "free gifts of love," Taylor and I sat on a blanket in front of them and enjoyed engaging in the atmosphere around us while viewing the festival from a slightly different perspective. There was a pile of wet wipes next to us on the ground, so I grabbed one and began wiping down my feet in a half-assed attempt to clean the evidence left behind from camping in the wilderness the night before. Produced in less than five minutes, the man handed me a white 3x5 notecard with the following words:

> *the dirt on our feet*
> *tracks our progress as we walk*
> *from home to sweet home*

> *for Karissa*

I felt so overjoyed when I read these words. I had been toiling and contemplating moving home, yet I wasn't sure if I was ready. I wasn't sure if I had finished what I had set out to experience in Ohio. Although I felt at home in the Midwest, I knew I also felt at home in Nevada. I was torn and confused, tormented and taunted by witnessing the lives of others and constantly asking myself, "What does *my* home look like? Where do *I* belong?"

This poem answered my question. It fulfilled me in a way, reassuring me it was okay to have multiple homes and reiterating that home is a feeling, not a place. The poem told me I could carry my homes with me, that the dirt on my feet would track the miles I've gone. Oh, those words on that day, in that place, during that time of my inner battle, were perfect. I still have them hanging on my corkboard above my desk. And as I've continued to live a sort of transient life, I have never again asked myself where my home is; I know now that it dwells within me. It is the integrity and character I carry. It is how I choose to love and treat myself as well as other people. It is the relationships I foster and nourish. It is my heart, mind, soul, spirit, and body all wrapped up together in this life— that is my home. And as for the physical world, I have many sweet homes, and for that, I am blessed.

Like Pip in *Great Expectations* and Dorothy in *The Wonderful Wizard of Oz*, after the whirlwind of an adventure and the conquering satisfaction of sought-after curiosity, our hearts long to take us back to the familiar, back to who we once were and what we once believed. We can never unlearn the magical knowledge of experience, but we can carry our new perspectives with us, plant new seeds of hopes and dreams, and harvest a completely new crop of imagination, influence, and adventure. And from time to time, when I find myself feeling lost in it all, I look back up at the corkboard and remember how I felt in that moment, to receive those words. All over again, I feel gratified.

As both a dreamer and a doer, I wanted to make the most of every moment that summer. Since I had been gone from Nevada for some time, my friends and I planned an ambitious camping trip in late July. We hauled ten people and eleven dogs to a secluded spot in the Stanislaus National Forest that housed two beautiful lakes and an endless array of mountains and hiking trails. We all set up our own sites within earshot of one another, and we made a communal area for dining, drinking, and conversing. To our delight, the entire campground was rather vacant, and the weather was exactly what you'd hope for when you head out for a summer camping trip.

Leave it to me, though, to find the other few and far between campers. In the early morning hours, I walked around the campsites, sharing neighborly conversations with other campers who were up for engaging with a stranger. I found myself in conversation with a vivacious couple with whom I shared my story about my Nevada roots and Ohio enterprise. I explained to them the uncertainty of my current situation, and I also informed them of my goal to Katniss Everdeen a deer from horseback. They seemed to take to my spice of life, and the woman eagerly explained to me that her middle son would "just love me." She explained that he was single, a hunter, and a train conductor who lived in Utah and that he was about my age. I gave her my social media information and told her to pass it along, as I've never been opposed to making new friends virtually either.

When we returned home from our outing, I received an unpretentious message from a Kyle G. Halverson. He was funny, friendly, and full of life. He had an incredible passion for hunting, a feat I was newly exposed to, and he was well versed in the ways of the land. He traveled all over the country to hunt different animals, and when he heard I lived on farm in Ohio infested with white-tailed deer, he was ecstatic. We forged an unlikely friendship over the phone, and to my pleasure, our connection evolved into another exciting story—don't worry; I'll get to that.

While "vacationing" in Nevada that summer, I was fortunate to receive yet another appealing invitation for excitement and travel. This emprise was to my family's yearly reunion in Key West, Florida. Most of my mother's family resided in the Sunshine State, so we West-Coasters often missed the opportunity to attend. Since it became a regular event for the family to go to Key West during the kickoff week of lobster season, the Floridians were more familiar with the sport of lobstering than I was. However, it was during the previous summer that I had learned the ropes of diving for the delectable bottom-feeders that have become such a delicacy in our society. When I had proven my skills to dive and catch lobsters, my uncle deemed me the "ocean slayer." This was a title I wore with pride and

I'm pretty sure that is why my uncle offered to pay my way to join the crew again. I think he mainly wanted me to be a part of the endeavor so his bounty would increase, but, needless to say, I didn't hesitate to jump on this ten-day vacation from my vacation.

So, after the camping extravaganza, my brother and I made arrangements for the dogs and planned a round-trip adventure that would eventually take us both from Nevada to Florida and back again. I flew out a few days before my brother and stayed with my uncle who foot the bill in order to help him prepare for the boat-hauling road trip, which would only take us about four hours. He utilized my presence to do some grocery shopping, errand running, gear cleaning, and meal prepping; undoubtedly, I put my best foot forward and gratefully assisted.

We caught over 250 lobsters that trip. We spent early mornings and long days diving into the ocean, and cool nights around hot meals and cold drinks, catching up on our lives. Spending time with my uncles, aunts, and cousins reminded me of the keen bonds I'd developed in Ohio and what it all really meant to me. I'd become a part of this family there, and I'd established a life for myself that I thoroughly enjoyed. Although the original attraction of moving to a farm evolved into a journey of self-discovery, I realized I was excited to return to the Midwest. I missed my people—not to mention, I was looking forward to contributing my hand-caught lobster for a little surf 'n' turf Ohio feast.

But when I returned from the ocean-slaying vacation, my theoretical plans were met with what could be deemed as another dead end. When I had first planned to drive home with Jill, I simply figured I would catch a one-way flight back to Ohio. To my dismay, no airline would allow me to ship my dogs on a plane in the heat of summer, so that option quickly flew out the window. I wracked my brain, as well as those of my confidants, to find an option to get the three of us back to Ohio for under a thousand dollars. As crunch time approached, things were looking grim until I was able to find a one-way car-rental for less than four hundred bucks. Score! I would soon be off to mission across the country for technically the fourth time that summer, but this time, it was just me and my dogs making the trip via four wheels.

When the time came for me to hit the road and head back to Ohio, Kyle G. Halverson offered to put me up in Utah for my first night's journey. And I hardly ever turn down a free place to stay, so I, of course, agreed. My stay at his home was cozy, comical, and comfortable. I know what you're thinking. "C'mon, Karissa, what if he turned out to be a murderer or some creepy old man on the sex offender list?" And to that I'd say, sometimes you just have to take a leap of faith. Kyle G. Halverson was a perfect gentleman that night; he made no advances toward me, other than offering me beer and pizza in his little one-bedroom apartment. And since he's such a gentleman, he let the dogs and me take his room while he slept on the couch. He promised me that having us stay in his home didn't cramp his style, and he woke up to see us off before sunrise the next day.

On day two, I made it about nine hours and then crashed with my cousin who lived just outside of Denver, Colorado. We arrived early enough that I was even able to take my fur-babies to a dog-friendly bar and have a drink with another friend who lived in the area. The third day, I had no plans to meet anyone or stay anywhere, so I just drove until I felt like stopping. I was a little nervous, but thanks to my father, the loaded .38 under my seat comforted me well enough. I pulled off into a hotel outside of St. Louis just after the sun went down. I was beat, and as soon as I got into bed, I was out like a light. I didn't leave the room until the sun rose the next morning to continue on my way.

By day four, I was back in Tennessee where I had left my truck with my mom just about ten weeks prior. By now you know detours are kind of my thing, and, well, since I had been in touch with Annie about my timeline throughout the summer, we worked out a fun meetup on her property in Virginia for the tail end of my trip. Her family owned some land in the serendipitous Shenandoah Valley. So, on my route back to Ohio, we coordinated a weekend for Annie, Cindy, and me to stay at their house in Virginia. However, this house was no fancy vacation home. It was more like a quaint cabin on a picturesque hillside, equipped with running water, electricity, and just enough blankets and living supplies for our brief recess.

The charm and warmth of this place allowed for peacefulness and tranquility to reign. After spending a summer apart, it was the perfect place to recapture our bond. This cottage was a place the Reynolds loved to retreat to, as they had owned it for a number of years. Annie recalled fond memories of spending weekends of her childhood there. They kept a rotation of cattle on the pasturelands throughout the warmer months of the year, so not only was it a regular getaway for them, but oftentimes, they would still have to work when they were there. For this trip though, Annie planned for recreation.

We spent the first hours relaxing and doing yoga guided by Cindy on the grass in front of the house. Then, Annie and I made our way through a nearby local fair and onto a tiny, local cider brewery that actually made cider from some of the apple trees on their property. We signed up for a cider tasting and enjoyed the knowledge and hospitality provided while we sipped the various suds. We each purchased a few bottles before we departed. That night, Annie, Cindy, and I drove to a nearby town named

Staunton to partake in a community affair filled with live music, local food, and fun festivities.

These brief days with two women I had come to admire and love so greatly washed away any remaining doubt I had about returning to Ohio. They were a solid reminder that I was certainly still happy to be in the Midwest. I mean, so what things hadn't unfolded as I'd imagined they would. The truth was, I was eager to return to the Reed farm, the slaughterhouse, and the steakhouse. My work in Ohio wasn't done yet, and I still had some growing to do.

Changed

After my "summer vacation," I couldn't wait to dive back into my life in Ohio. I wanted to focus on crossing a few goals off my bucket list and redefining some old dreams that had fallen by the wayside. At this point, I had no idea where the winds of change might take me, but I wanted to be sure I was still accomplishing some of the things I had set out to do.

My Bucket List

-Kill a deer with a bow; dress and process it myself
-Take ballroom dancing lessons
-Go on a solo overnight backpacking excursion
-Sew my own outfit
-Write a book
-See Chicago and New York
-Go to Europe

I had forged this list before I even moved to Ohio, and at first, I had been so overwhelmed with the excitement and newness of being outside of my comfort zone that I didn't focus too much on achieving any of my goals during that first year. However, when I returned to the Midwest and decided I would stay on the Reed farm, I opted to make the most of my new life, and I brought the list back out. By this time, I had written and printed my first book, which was a small spiritual devotional. Though, if I'm being honest, even that accomplishment had its own waves because it all came into fruition when my mom was visiting me in Ohio.

I've always journaled my feelings and personal prayers as a way of expressing myself. I'd compiled detailed events of fun experiences and cathartically made my way through trying times page by page. One time, when my mom came to visit me, she asked if she could read through some of the diaries I had lying out in my room. She was my mother, and she knew all of my trials and most of the feelings that went along with them, so I didn't hesitate to give her permission. I did warn her that there might be a thing or two about her inside, so she had to promise not to get upset if there was anything that rubbed her the wrong way. I didn't think much of it at the time, although she encouraged me that my words were inspiring and that I should share them with others.

It wasn't until sometime later, when I was visiting her in Tennessee, that I discovered a whole stack of photocopied versions of my journals in her home.

"Umm, hello!? What the hell is this? Are these my journals?" I screamed when I discovered the binder full of copies of my personal thoughts.

"What? Oh, honey, they are so good!" she replied, trying to defend herself.

"What the hell!? Did you steal my journals?"

"Well, you said I could read them. I just wanted to have my own copies," she pleaded.

"Without asking me?!" I was livid.

"Hold on a minute, honey."

"No, Mom, *you* hold on! These are private! I don't even know what's in there—and you made *copies*!"

"Baby, they're so good! I just want to show you something."

I took a deep breath, trying to keep the raging storm within me at bay. Defensively, I watched as she showed me a group of pages she'd put together and highlighted. I was not impressed or pleased, to say the least. *How could she do that to me?* I felt exposed and vulnerable as I saw my words and feelings in my own handwriting being presented to me. She reassured me that no one else had seen them, though part of me didn't believe her.

"Honey, these are so good. I pulled out the ones I really liked, and look," she ushered me to come sit by her and look at my own personal journals again, "if you put them together like this, they could be like a little book of prayers."

I was annoyed. Again, unimpressed. In fact, I was so furious that I packed my truck in the next few minutes and told her I was leaving back to Ohio that night instead of the next day as I'd planned. I threatened her, saying I wouldn't speak to her again if she showed anyone my thoughts.

But as it turned out, later, I actually was glad she did this. Hindsight is my only explanation, but by actually seeing a compiled and organized outside perspective of those pages, I was able to envision the book that could be born from them. Mothers. Somehow, they always know—even if we aren't always willing to see what they see at first. This compilation is what later became my first book, titled, *Today, I Pray.*

That devotional is actually what propelled me to write this book. I realized I could apply the same timely process of organizing and editing my thoughts and words to my dream of composing another book. At this time, I didn't know exactly what my story would be, but I kept writing and thinking and contemplating and trying. I just didn't have my story—yet.

By mid-Autumn, I was back into the swing of things in Ohio. I worked a lot and spent my spare time enjoying the calls of my heart: developing my skills with my beloved bow, partaking in outdoor endeavors aligned with the harvest season, and spending quality time with those wonderful Ohio souls.

With permission from the Reeds and the Reynolds, I had invited Kyle G. Halverson out for some white-tailed shenanigans. Along with his playful demeanor and obvious charm, Mr. G. Halverson dignifiedly referred to himself in the third person, always using his full name. Once our friendship blossomed, I learned that I, too, loved to refer to my new buddy as, in fact, the one, the only, Kyle G. Halverson. He came to Ohio to hunt and stay for just over a week in early November. I picked him up at the airport in Columbus, and we made a quick pit stop at Cabela's so he could purchase a license and any gear he needed. We drove out to my humble abode, and I excitedly gave him a tour of the Reed's property. He didn't hesitate to talk with the neighbors and local hunters about where to scout the deer he craved to catch. Although, with no luck after a few days at the Reed farm, we made our way down to Annie's house so he could try his hand on her property.

Once again, he scouted and read the land and spoke with Thomas and Bruce to get a better idea of where he could land a kill shot. I still had to work, so some of the days he was on his own, however I was determined to hunt with him when I could. He wasn't used to the type of hunting the Midwest offered, but he was a huntsman, so he naturally purveyed this prospective land. One night, while I was with him, he spotted a small heard upwind from where we stood. He explained how this worked to our benefit as they might not smell or hear us coming. With stealth, he got into position and aimed his bow. His arrow flung into the air with no avail. He almost got one, but his arrow missed. Discouraged, he thought that would be the last opportunity for him to score. As a hunter, he was used to defeat, and he reassured me that it was all part of the sport.

In good spirits, we decided to show him how the country folk on this side of the Mississippi get rowdy. Again, I had to work, so I showed up late to the party at a local country bar that night. When I arrived, Kyle was on the more inebriated side of life. He certainly had himself a grand ole time. The next morning, well, we'll just say all Kyle G. Halverson wanted was a greasy cheeseburger. On a quest to help him land some kind of meat, a few of us made our way to the Elm Tree Pub for a late lunch. We devoured our burgers, and because our Utah amigo wasn't feeling ship-shape that day, we headed back to the house so he could sleep off the rest of his hangover.

We pulled into the driveway around 3:00 p.m., and lo and behold, there were two deer some twenty yards away from the garage, grazing on the grass where the edge of the property met the woods. Annie pointed them out.

"Hey, Kyle, you see the deer?" she announced.

In a bit of a daze he replied, "Well, looky there!" His faced lit up instantly.

"Pull in slow," Annie told me. "Park down by the pool. You guys can go in through the basement, grab your bows, and then come out through the garage."

That girl is a genius, I tell you what. We did just as she said, grabbing our gear and quietly making our way through the house and out the garage door. We quickly got set up, both drawing back our bows, and then Kyle looked at me, nodding for me to take the shot. I had never shot at an animal like this before, and I was filled with nerves. This was an easy, broadside shot, seemingly all too perfect, and the deer froze. Even though I'm pretty sure I could have done it successfully, it was Kyle's last day, and he had surely put his hours in that week without reward. I rested my bow and gave him the green light.

Thwap! The sound of his release was met with the glory he'd been waiting for. After a few minutes, he tracked the trail of blood left by the animal and found him in the bushes just a few yards away. What a way to end his trip! He sobered up instantly as the endorphins and glee revamped his spirit. Right there, we dressed the animal and hauled the mammal to a tree in Annie's front yard to drain the blood and skin the carcass. Kyle let me get my hands dirty as he walked me through the process; it was the same as what I was used to at the slaughterhouse, but this time, we were in the rugged outdoors! Mission complete.

The whole ordeal didn't take more than a half hour or so, but we basked in the delight of a job well done. Annie sat with us and watched as we cleaned up the mess we'd made. She snapped some photos of us indulging in the process and a few of me posing with our bounty. Her little kitten, Jim Beam, even made his way over to investigate the situation and lick the innards that apparently tasted good to the tiny feline. My favorite picture from that day was of little Jimmy, his face smeared with blood, posing with a fiendish glare.

I called George to ask if we could use the slaughterhouse to finish processing the meat. He cheerfully invited us to bring the carcass to the slaughterhouse that night to hang in the cooler and told us I could come back to butcher it the next day. Since he too was an avid hunter, it was his pleasure to help us out. George lived in walking distance from the slaughterhouse, so he invited us over to show off his collection of trophy animals. The game he hunted was much bigger than what Kyle was familiar with, nevertheless, the two bonded momentarily over their shared passion, and it served to be the perfect send-off for Kyle.

The next day, after taking Kyle to the airport, I went to back to Lee's to process and wrap the deer. After a few days in the deep freezer, I'd be able to ship it to Kyle. Let me tell you, white-tailed deer that graze on fields of oat and corn sure taste a lot better than the sagebrush-eating mule deer he was used to in Utah.

"That was the most expensive deer I've ever killed," Kyle joked. "But hot-dang is it good eatin'!" he informed me after he had made his first meal out of the meat.

The pleasure in his voice was affirmation for me that, once again, forging connections with strangers can turn into joys beyond our imaginations. I mean, I had randomly met his mother in the wilderness on a beautiful, summer morning, and less than four months later, an unlikely adventure was had. I am constantly amazed by the unraveling of life and the excitement that can come in unorthodox ways.

Shortly after his visit, my friend Charlotte from back home flew out to Chicago to meet me for a quick weekend getaway. We decided to meet in Chi-Town because she was ready for a vacation and it was on my list of places I wanted to visit. Chicago was only a five-hour car drive from Columbus, so I figured it would behoove me to check it out while I lived so close. Although after configuring the details of our trip, I opted to fly instead. There was no sense in trying to maneuver my big truck through the city, and by flying, I was able to optimize my time there with my bestie. We only had three short days to see the city, and we'd planned our endeavor around a concert of our favorite hip-hop group: Atmosphere—you know, the same group we had chased around California.

We had fun exploring the city and seeing what there was to see during the cold season in late November. We had been reassured a number of times that the city was livelier in the summer, but we didn't care. To our pleasure, my boss at Smith and Wollensky arranged for us to have dinner at the sister restaurant in Chicago. We were warmly welcomed with a tour of the facility and seated at a highly desired table surrounded by beautiful paintings and nestled in front of a floor-to-ceiling window with a view. The building sat right on the river, and illuminated skyscrapers served as our backdrop while we dined on assorted cheese and sizzling steaks suitably paired with champagne and Burgundy. It was to our surprise that when the bill arrived, the waiter informed us, "Your money is no good here."

Now that was the icing on our cake! I couldn't believe it at the time, but my manager at Smith and Wollensky had somehow comped our entire meal. We didn't know it when we ordered the abundance of food and top-shelf wine, but it certainly made us feel pretty special. The next day, we galivanted through the city, eating our way through the recommended pizza and hot dog hotspots. We strolled by the Bean and local parks as many sightseers do. That evening, we took the public railway to the concert venue and hip-hopped our feet off into the wee hours of the morn. Exhausted and slightly intoxicated, we made our way back to the hotel. We were due to leave the next day and couldn't help but feel relaxed, rejuvenated, and completely content with our three-day flight of fancy.

I was stoked to cross basically another two dreams off my bucket list. When I returned from Chicago back to Columbus, the restaurant was due to be busy through the Thanksgiving weekend. I was blessed to have a lot of fun in the previous weeks, so I knew it would be time to grind again now that the holiday season was upon us. I'd learned the previous year that it was during the holidays the money at the steakhouse rolled in. I told my bosses I was so grateful for all of the time off they had given me that year, so not to hesitate to schedule me double-shifts, seven days a week. I was eager to show them my commitment, not to mention excited to refill my depleted savings account.

And then it happened. December 6, 2016. A day I'll never forget. The ultimate wrench was thrown into my newly hatched plans when I saw my bloody digit fly through the air and land in the corner of the room on the cement floor of the slaughterhouse. I was mortified, and everything changed.

Exposure

I went back to the slaughterhouse for the first time on February 3, 2017, two short months after amputating my thumb. It was pretty emotional. I cried shortly after pulling into the parking area. I started to feel anxious and choked up, so I called my dad.

"Hello," I sobbed as I tried to greet him over the phone.

"Hey kid, are you okay?" he asked in an instantly concerned tone.

"Yeah," I barely uttered as I tried to maintain my composure, even though I had none.

"What's going on?" my dad tried to get me to speak. "Is everything all right Karissa?"

"Yeah, I'm okay," I tearfully said. "I'm…at…" I took a hesitant breath, "the slaughterhouse."

My patient father waited for me to go on. I would often call my dad when I was in an emotionally overwhelmed state, so he was quite proficient at dealing with his distressed daughter. He was used to this behavior of mine since I was a teenager; but more specifically in the weeks following my injury, he probably knew that I was calling because I was upset or distraught rather than calling because of an actual emergency.

I finally mustered my composure enough to relay the reason why I was calling. My voice was still broken as I uttered, "I'm scared."

"I bet you are. You don't have to do this you know," he spoke softly. "It's going to be pretty traumatic."

I am the one who decided I needed to go back to the slaughterhouse. For weeks I'd been reliving that

174

dreadful day over and over again in my mind: seeing broken images of my thumb detached from my hand, a hazy array of medical professionals tending to me and the distressed onlookers who were near me during that horrific incident. I often heard the recurring noise of the ambulance's siren ringing in my head and eerie words like 'catastrophic,' 'traumatic,' and 'emergency' repeated in my mind. By that point in time, almost any sudden noise would trigger the sound of the bandsaw in my mind and send tension and stress throughout my body. It could be the coffee grinder, a lawnmower or even a sound from a movie that would trigger agonizing feelings that caused uneasy emotions to flood my being.

"Just breathe kid, it's not going to be easy," he reassured me as I listened. "You're probably going to freeze when you get inside. Just walk slowly and take your time. Does your boss know you are coming?"

"Yes," I muttered.

"Good. Is Annie going to be there?"

"I don't know. She said she'd try to make it if she could," I replied.

"Well hopefully she shows up. You will probably feel better if she's there," he encouraged me. "Now when you get inside, if you don't want to be there, you can leave okay?"

"Okay," I softly sobbed.

"Your mind is probably going to tell you that you can't handle it, but just tell yourself you are going to be okay. Just repeat those words 'Everything is going to be okay.' Okay? Let me hear you say it," he prodded.

"I'm going to be okay," I said disinterestedly.

"Now remember, you don't have to do this. You can leave at any point. It's okay to get upset and it's okay to leave, okay?"

175

"Okay," I started to gain a bit of self-assurance. "Thanks dad. I love you."

"I love you too, Kris. You are going to do great. You can call me after if you need to okay?"

"Okay, thanks," I breathed a heavy sigh.

Once I hung up the phone, I got out of the truck and saw George waiting for me in his truck. He promptly got out and noticed my tear-filled eyes. Almost immediately, his eyes welled up too.

He quickly turned back around and opened the passenger door of his truck. He reached in for some meat I'd requested for a Galentine's Day celebration with my girlfriends, saying he'd better get it to me before he forgot. I thanked him, and I fought to hold back tears as I walked the tenderloin over to my truck, quickly opened the door, and then tossed it in.

Let's get this over with, I thought to myself as I took a deep breath and turned around to head inside the glass door with the open sign, as usual, hanging a little crooked. I felt myself get worked up by just picturing the emergency vehicles I'd seen the last time I was in front of the building. *Just breathe.*

We walked in the door, and I could no longer hold it together. I finally let it all out. It was difficult remembering it all—the accident, the emotions I had felt during the trying days of recovery, and the faint glimmer of hope I once owned when I had first walked through those precious slaughterhouse doors.

I had loved working there. Learning to cut and process meat had quickly become a passion of mine; it simultaneously gave me answers and invoked more questions in me. I was fascinated to learn the different ways to identify a healthy carcass, and I loved eating fresh meat for lunch on days we ran the kettle. I never would have thought being a butcher would be something that

176

could fill me up so completely, but this passion bloomed within me, like a meadow of wild flowers; I was meant for this. I was challenged and captivated, and it aligned with my circumstances and skill set.

But all of that love had faded after my accident. The trauma had tainted things for me, stolen my drive. I didn't want to identify as a butcher anymore. I couldn't. I just wanted to be Karissa, the girl full of passion and life, the girl who, as of late, didn't seem to exist anymore.

I looked around the shop. The machinery, the cement floors, the smell of raw meat—all of it used to energize me, but now, I just felt shut off, cold, indifferent. A sense of uneasiness still stirred in my stomach, and we hadn't even reached the back room where the bandsaw stood.

"This is hard," I cried to George.

"I know. I bet, but I'll do whatever you need me to do," he comforted me.

I swallowed hard and took a deep breath. I looked up for Annie and said, "I wish Annie was here." My voice cracked, and I welled up with tears again, but I walked back toward the saw anyway. "Do the guys know I'm here?"

"No. They don't, sweetie," George replied.

It upset me to hear that because I didn't want to be a distraction or have a dramatic entrance, but I couldn't help it.

We entered the room where I'd spent hours cutting, wrapping, boning, weighing, packing, and sawing. I looked over to the corner of the room where I had once seen my thumb on the floor. The image of that traumatic moment was engraved in my mind. I knew I had to change that wretched image. I had to face it. I had to get back on the metaphorical horse. I knew I needed to get the initial exposure over with in order to move on.

I walked toward the saw, and all four guys welcomed me with smiles on their faces and slight surprise in their eyes. It had been a couple months since I'd been around, and the last time they had seen me was when I cut my thumb off. Actually, I guess they had seen me one other time when I made a drug-induced appearance at the Christmas party with my mom as my escort. Truthfully, though, I don't remember much of that night, as it was only a week or so after the accident.

After a few minutes, I was able to gather some fortitude, and I even showed off my little Thumbelina. For a few moments, a few of us held our thumbs out to compare butcher battle scars, and we laughed and agreed that I was by far the winner.

"I don't want to be the winner of that competition," I shyly commented.

We all laughed.

I turned to the bandsaw and said, "Hello, old friend. Remember me?" I was terrified, but I forced myself to act confident. Fake it 'til you make it, right?

I stood in the same exact place I had stood a few months prior. My feet felt cemented to the floor. *You can do this,* I encouraged myself.

The room was silent, and I could feel all eyes on me, even though a few guys remained dutifully working their tasks.

I turned the saw on. It roared with power. Adrenaline rushed through my chest, down my arms, and out my fingertips. My legs were numb. I felt my eyes close, but I forced them open and quickly hit the button to turn the machine off. I let out a sigh, releasing the stress I had been holding in. I announced it would probably be a few more months before I felt the desire to cut a pork shoulder again.

I wasn't afraid (or so I told myself.) I was just emotional. I didn't want to make small talk, and I didn't want to be there long. I turned to Howie with a voice full of gratitude and sincerity, and I muttered, "Thank you for picking up my thumb and taking care of me that day. And thanks for calling Annie."

"I'm used to working with meat and bone. That one was just a little smaller," he joked and then shot me a smile. "It was not a problem at all, missy. I'm just glad they were able to get it back on! It's looking pretty dang good too!"

I smiled timidly, but I wanted to leave, so I made it known. It was all I could handle for the day, and I walked out rather promptly. My dad had given me permission ahead of time to just leave when I was done, so that's just what I did.

Phew. That part is over, I thought to myself as I pulled away. I began to cry again, but not because I was burdened. I was happy. I was happy to have new images of the slaughterhouse in my mind—smiling faces from all of my sweet coworkers and a bandsaw that no longer had the last word. I was still haunted by the reality of my injury, but I was one step closer to overcoming the mental challenges I was facing. And I knew I'd be back.

Hope

On one of my first follow-up visits after the initial surgery, the hand surgeon told me the recovery time for this kind of injury was six months to a year. I aimed to be better before that. When they told me to do thirty exercises a day, I did ninety. No joke. When they told me to rest and avoid certain things like caffeine and cold weather, I followed their prescriptions to a T. He informed me that the first one to three months would be the hardest. And boy, was he right.

I slowly began to adjust to the inability to use my thumb. I couldn't pick anything up with my left hand. It turns out these opposable thumbs come in handy for a thing—or seven—in life. Try to imagine not being able to use your thumb for anything. Yeah, it's not easy, but I was thankful it wasn't my right thumb.

The limitations didn't stop at picking things up either. I experienced excruciating pain with any movement; even a slight motion in my hand would send piercing pain up my arm. At first, I couldn't even bathe myself adequately. I couldn't put on my socks by myself. Hooking a bra on my own was definitely out of the question. I struggled to put on most of my jewelry, even though both my mother and Bee insisted I adorn my loose-fitting outfits with jewelry to help boost my confidence. I quickly accepted that I had to receive assistance when eating certain meals. Luckily, my mom was there in the beginning weeks of my recuperation to help me with these tasks. But with every day that passed, my stubborn nature pushed me to do more than I thought I could without aid. I started to use my other fingers when I could tolerate redeveloping the habitual motions of using my left hand. I got used to eating sandwiches tucked in between my left index and middle fingers—well, at least just using it as a support for my dominant right hand. I was told that with these kind of injuries, humans adapt, so I was adapting.

My mom still tells the story of me attempting to eat a Chipotle burrito when we first left the hospital. I struggled to get the beast of a burrito stable in my hands. Frustrated, I instead plopped it on the table in front of me with enough force to flatten the bottom and have it stand propped up, basically on its own. With my right hand as a stabilizer, I just bent over, opened my mouth and went to town, literally eating every bite behemoth-style right there in the middle of the restaurant. If I had to adjust to this injury, so could any judging onlookers.

I had an incredible amount of support offered by everyone around the farm. Bee made me breakfast every morning, graciously hollering up the stairs and asking if I wanted oatmeal, Cream of Wheat, or eggs. She knew the healing power of a hot meal. She also fed my dogs breakfast every day, and there were no complaints from them as Bee was known to add in extra bits of leftovers and yogurt to their kibble. They loved grandma Bee as much as I did. When I made my infrequent debuts downstairs, Pop would encourage me to talk about my day and my feelings, even if I didn't have much to say. He'd ask me how I was feeling and listen to my words, nudging puzzle pieces my way and encouraging me to help find their places. On the days he could tell I was really struggling, he'd remind me of one of our inside jokes or tease me by asking me to do some outlandish task he knew I couldn't. He always knew how to pull a smile out of me.

So you can see why these relationships were the elixirs to my agony and uncertainty.

Juke had come to the hospital every single day while I was in recovery on the replant floor of Riverside.

He'd bring his son, some of my favorite food, or a mix of music for my enjoyment. He showed up at the farm regularly to make sure his helping hands were utilized for Pop and Bee, and also for my mother and me. He insisted that Bee put him to work whether it was taking out the trash, running an errand, or fixing the rail of the staircase. One day, he showed up with a Christmas tree, without being asked, and insisted that he set it up. He cherished the holiday season, and he was determined to make it a brighter time for all than it seemingly was. Bee jokingly referred to him as Saint Nick due to his relentless, jolly, and spirited presence.

The first month of my rehabilitation, I practiced a daily regime of routinely popping painkillers and baby aspirin and then sleeping. The farm was flooded with activity due to the encroaching holiday season as the extended family began to arrive for their vacations. I intentionally stayed tucked away in my quarters, usually only making an appearance downstairs during mealtimes. Even then, I wasn't much for conversation or liveliness like I typically would have been. Thankfully, everyone was so preoccupied with their own business that much wasn't expected of me either.

It wasn't that I didn't enjoy seeing the familiar faces of the family members I'd come to know over the past couple of years while living in Ohio. And believe me when I say my bizarre accident proved to be the perfect tale for wisecracks and one-liners about a nine-fingered lady and misplaced digits. I actually loved the sense of ease it gave me knowing others could joke about it. To me, that meant I must be doing okay. I too had been making jokes about the incident since the ambulance ride. And trust me, over the course of those first few weeks, I heard 'em all! From the get-go, I received gifts of thumb-puppets, a thumb wrestling ring, about a thousand thumbs-up emojis, and nicknames like Thumpkin and Thumbelina. But still, it was hard for me to see all the family with their holiday spirits, exhausting even. I was struggling, in the depths of a depression, and seeing everyone only reminded me how much I wasn't myself.

At the six-week mark, I was permitted to mild exercise. For me, this was a huge blessing because I'd been an active runner and exercise enthusiast for many years. Not having this outlet as a means for emotional release was frustrating for me, even though I lacked the energy for it. Still, being told you can't do something just adds that much more sting to the situation. Needless to say, when I got the green light to work out, I looked for a gym close to the farm where I could spend some focused time on my healing. I found a small, local place where the owners welcomed me with open arms to come in, heal, and get myself well at my own pace. Once they heard my story, they even waived the initial seventy-five-dollar fee and encouraged me to pay just a simple ten dollars a month. This was yet another tiny blessing for me on the road to recovery, especially since I wasn't able to work.

I went to the gym almost daily between weeks six and ten. It was so encouraging for me to practice grabbing bars, ropes, pulleys, and weights with my left hand. I would test my limits to see what I could do and what pain I could withstand. Do to the fact that my schedule was rather open, I often enjoyed the solitude in the gym and the freedom to use the equipment as I attempted to gain momentum and strength. One time, however, I went in the evening hours and the place was packed. Although I did enjoy chatting with a few folks during the busy time, I found being there when it was quiet was more conducive to my healing.

Routinely, I needed to drive to Columbus a few times a week for various appointments: physical therapy, psychological counseling, and regular checkups with my surgeon. After the initial weeks of being laid up on the farm, I was happy for the busyness these appointments demanded. I grew close with my team of therapists throughout my weekly visits to the Hand Center. It was there I met others who suffered pretty serious hand injuries, including a man who actually had a toe-thumb, and it reminded me to keep things in perspective. My injury was certainly not the worst. Naturally, I tried to encourage others as I'd listen to their narratives and tragedies; subsequently, I too received healing encouragement from those who shared their stories and perspectives. Before long, I started to feel comfortable with where I was at in my process. There's something about knowing you aren't alone that can make things feel less intimidating.

I started making an effort to see a friend or two or to stop by the steakhouse to socialize for a bit while passing through the city. It was heartbreaking to not see these people on a regular basis, although I did have many people take the forty-minute drive out to the farm to visit me, bring me treats, and check on me those first few months. Rachel was my most frequent visitor. Sometimes, she'd spend hours with me, allowing me to get lost in deep conversation about the tumultuous feelings that raged within me. Or she would just drop off freshly baked goods with an encouraging note from time to time, which pleased my roommates as well. Bee joked how I must love all the attention I was getting; she wasn't wrong, but considering the situation, I would have opted not to be in this mess.

I was suffering a lot of pain in my left hand and felt physically weak much of the time—a malaise K-busy was certainly not used to. I struggled with feeling so restricted, so tied down, especially in an environment that used to bring out my most adventurous side. However, it seemed that whenever I'd start to get pulled too deep, the weight of my injury threatening to drown me, I'd receive a text, social media message, or letter of encouragement in the mail that would boost my spirits at just the right time.

One day, I got a phone call from my amazing friend Andrew Busch, who I worked with at the steakhouse, inviting me to join him and some of his friends to bowl before one of my physical therapy appointments.

"Hey, girly! A few of us are going bowling at eleven if you want to join," Andrew extended in his friendly manner.

"That sounds fun, but I'm not sure I can bowl," I bashfully replied.

"Well, why don't you just come hang with us for a bit. It'd be good to see you," he encouraged.

I decided I should go, and when I showed up, I realized I didn't know any of the guys he was with. But Andrew, standing up at his six-four height with a smile on his face, welcomed me with a big bear hug that lifted me off my feet. He then told his friends a little about my background and injury. Almost instantly, my splints and bandages were coming off to show the wounds on my hand. I nervously revealed to them my scars, but to my surprise, all of the guys were impressed and expressed care and concern.

"Holy shit! That was on the ground!" one of the guys exclaimed.

"Damn, girl! That looks like it hurt," another replied.

I nodded sheepishly. A twinge of embarrassment ran through me as this was the first time I'd shown any strangers my hand. But the more they looked, the more I realized they didn't care. Not even a bit. If anything, it made them kinder toward me. And soon, that embarrassment turned to empowerment. It really wasn't that big of a deal after all.

"Well, grab a ball, girly! Let's get you on the board," Andrew chimed in.

And, as it turned out, you don't really need your left hand to bowl. Or to play darts. Or even to be a half-assed goalie in foosball. This venture was the beginning of a time where I began to step away from the confines of my tiny comfort zone and once again step into opportunities of the unknown. I began to see just what else I could do with my newfound limitations and perspective.

After that day, a few of us started a weekly bowling league of our own. We met up every Tuesday and played for hours, though it was mostly about socializing and laughing. These Tuesday afternoons slowly began to remind me of the parallel grace that can exist during difficult times if you open up your heart and spirit to it. I became a better bowler during those months than I'd ever been before, and I slowly began gaining confidence in what I could do instead of focusing on what I couldn't do. Friends, even new ones, can be quite priceless.

To top it off, the guy who ran the counter at the bowling alley was quite a character. His name was Carl. He was probably in his late forties, and I'd come to learn that he had worked at the bowling alley for some twenty years. He was a cantankerous man who never smiled. His infrequent comments were usually garnished with words like shit-hole, shit-can, and goddamn. But he somehow always had my shoes in the correct size waiting for me on the counter when I arrived at eleven in the morning every Tuesday. At first, it baffled me, but eventually, it just made me assume there was a sweet man living beneath his gruffness. The reality was that he probably put the shoes on the counter so he could avoid having a conversation with this peppy girl from Nevada. For whatever reason, I loved the strange demeanor he possessed. It was so different than mine, but for where I was emotionally at the time, I felt like I wanted to adopt his back-the-hell-off attitude.

Cliff, who was one of the chefs that worked at Smith and Wollensky, also joined in on the regular Tuesday bowling league. Cliff and I had bonded at work because he had dreams of traveling to a new place, and I, in fact, was a person who'd done just this when I moved to Ohio. He was a bearded ginger with a dreamer's imagination and compassionate soul. He showed his consideration and understanding for my situation from the very start. He too drove out to the farm from time to time, not expecting my wellness or performance, but rather just making space for me as a concerned friend.

While in the early stages of my rehabilitation, Cliff had come over, and I wistfully ran through the list of all the things I could no longer do. I was in a low place, and he had listened. That night, he planted ideas of focusing on things I could do to encourage my situation. Shortly thereafter, he helped me obtain a Nintendo 64 so I could attempt to use the joystick to exercise my little Thumbelina. This became an activity I grew found of, even though I could only play for about ten minutes at a time before I felt worn out, both physically and mentally.

I had expressed to him how upset I was that I could no longer shuffle a deck of cards, so he thoughtfully did some YouTube research on different methods to shuffle a deck that didn't involve using both thumbs; from then on, we made regular attempts to get me back in the card-shuffling game. I quickly found that I wasn't very good at these adaptive methods, but the determination I had to be able to achieve this goal reminded me of my drive and creative resourcefulness. I left a deck out on a table in my room, and I would, time and time again, sit down, try, and fail to achieve this task. I'll never forget the moment when the cards fell into place. It was maybe my two hundredth attempt, but that gratifying moment when the deck aligned itself enough to not be considered a failure was the moment a ray of light glimmered on my situation. With focus, determination, and endurance, I could pick up the pieces of defeat and create tiny triumphs that pushed me forward on the road of recovery.

Around week thirteen, due to her own wavering set of circumstances, my mother decided to move back to Nevada. She asked if I was up for helping her take the cross-country drive, reassuring me that I wouldn't have to lift a finger. That truth was certainly exaggerated when the time for her to move actually came, but regardless, I was happy to be a part of the expedition. A dear soul, Brandon, who was a livestock hauler I'd met through Annie and had also become a close friend of mine, was kind enough to offer to drive me to Tennessee and drop me off so I could just fly straight back to Ohio after we made the haul across the country.

This would be my fourth drive between the Midwest and the West, and by now, I felt like a pro. My mom loved having my help and company, and I loved having another excuse to go home. It was also nice to have something meaningful to do with my time other than the now monotonous mild workouts, routine counseling, and physical therapy appointments. We were due to set sail the second week of March in 2017.

It just so happened that a few days before I left for Tennessee, I was invited to go see a play starring my friend Claire. I teamed up with Annie and Cindy to watch the musical performance in Lima. The after-party was held a few blocks away at a trendy bar and restaurant named Buckeye Brewery. The whole crew from the play was there celebrating the successful completion of their stunning

188

spectacle, and I jovially posted up at the bar, simply enjoying the energy in the air to my people-watching pleasure. A handsome man caught my eye throughout the evening. Turns out, Toby, as I learned was his name, happened to be the bar owner. We'd seen each other a few of times before when I would join the Reynolds for dinner or drinks at his establishment, but it wasn't until that night that I felt drawn to him in a physical way.

I kept my hand discreetly wrapped within my coat sleeve, so as to hide the brace I regularly wore. Toby had remembered my injury, and he courteously asked how I was doing with my recovery. It wasn't long before I realized he was giving me special attention, so I opted to increase the octaves of my charm. Toby resembled a lumberjack. He was muscular and had a bushy brown beard, and the more I talked to him, the more enamored I became.

Annie and I ended up staying until well beyond the bar's closing time that night, so Toby and his friend offered to take us to another place that was still open just a few doors down. Knowing I was due to leave for a few weeks, I didn't want the night to end. We stayed out until four in the morning. And somewhere amidst the subtle sips of Coors Light, it happened: Cupid's arrow blindsided me.

Ambition

I guess sometime before I left for another brief sabbatical to help my mom move back to Reno, Toby had attempted to contact me via Facebook, but I have never been a social media frequenter, so after not receiving a response from me, he acquired my phone number from Annie. She did ask for my permission first, which elated my heart with joy. Toby and I got to know each other over the phone while I was away. We shared long conversations from miles apart that served as a perfect foundation for our future relationship. When it was time for me to fly back to Ohio, he offered to pick me up at the airport. Let the marathon of fun dates and chemistry commence!

And fun, he was. From the moment he picked me up at the airport, he opened my eyes to a whole new world. He pulled me out of recovery mode and back into the swing of live-your-life-now mode. And the strange part was, being an enthusiastic extrovert wasn't even his personality. Something about our connection fueled an exciting light of life in each of us. He'd spent so many years meticulously building his business and not focusing on his personal life that the timing was perfect for us to calibrate each other to an elevated place in our lives. He was romantic, generous, hard-working, ridiculously smart, and occasionally blunt. I loved being toted around on his arm.

Since he owned his restaurant, he worked all the time. Having plenty of restaurant experience myself, I not only understood the demands of his job, but I complemented his skills, and we were able to talk about everything work-related with great understanding on both ends. He was thoughtful and scrupulous. When he made plans or had projects, he worked tirelessly to execute his aims with impressive attention to detail. He'd spend late nights perfecting his undertakings, and I would often sit with him while sipping some sour brew. When he wanted, I would dive right in and do the dirty work along with him.

On maybe our third date, we galivanted around Columbus, hopping from restaurant to bar to coffee shop to bar. He wanted to show me everywhere he loved to go, and he historically educated me about each venue's significance—in the city and in his heart. After having too much to drink, we decided to get a hotel room in Columbus. Our physical relationship hadn't quite escalated to the intimacy of sharing a bed, but let's face it, we were wasted, and driving was not an option. Around 11:00 p.m., we called around, looking for relatively inexpensive, adequate accommodations. We booked a room at the Hampton Inn and Suites near where we suckled on the local libations.

It was half-passed one when we finally made it to the hotel. We were met with annoyance when we checked in and the front desk worker told us that the hotel would not have running water until seven the next morning. The alcohol induced anger surged from my mouth as I took out my frustrations on the young employee. Toby was also rather intoxicated and exhausted, and he consoled both me and the young man who gave us the disheartening news that it would all be okay. He reassured me that we could just sleep until seven. The guy handed us a few Dasani water bottles to help ease our discontentment and told us not to hesitate to call the front desk if we needed anything.

I fell asleep fully clothed as soon as my head hit the pillow. I woke up in dire need of water around seven-thirty. I got up, chugged a few gulps, and plopped myself on the toilet to urinate the excess alcohol that my liver already processed. *You've got to be kidding me.* Mother nature

191

had decided to join me on that fateful morning, and I was ill-equipped for her surprise visit. Petrified, I attempted to erratically clean myself up without waking the handsome creature on the other side of the door. My bodily secretions covered my fingertips, and I stumbled over to the sink to clean my soiled hands. I turned the faucet on. Nothing happened. I tried to flush the toilet again in an effort to hide the evidence of my untimely visitor, but nope. Wasn't working. Embarrassed, I swiftly scurried out of the bathroom, grabbed one of the Dasani bottles, and then poured it on my hands. In my best attempt to be sanitary, I lathered up a perfectly clean white towel and quickly watched it fade to pink. *Are you kidding me right now? I hardly know this guy. And yet here I am. Why? Why now?!*

"Toby, are you awake?" I gently poked his shoulder.

He didn't budge.

I called the front desk to find out just what the hell was going on, and I sat in fear of humiliation, trying to ponder what to do next.

"I'm sorry, ma'am, but there was a problem with the water repairs overnight, and the water isn't due to be back on until 9:00 a.m." I hung up the phone, feeling pissed off, but not before I asked for a few more water bottles to be delivered to our room.

I laid back and quickly passed out again. This time, Toby woke me up and said he was going to be late for work if we didn't get our move on. He wanted to take me to breakfast and run a few errands in Columbus before his work meeting at noon. By this time, it was nine-thirty, and there was still no water. I told him about my phone conversation but hesitated to tell him about my personal ordeal. He could sense something was off, and after a few minutes of debating in my head how this would play out, I told him the awkward truth. I sat frozen as I waited for his reaction. You know what he did? He laughed and told me not to worry one bit. He did his best to comfort me, and he even helped pour some water on me from the other side of the shower curtain so I could feel more adequately cleaned up. With each passing moment and each pour of the water bottle, my fondness for him grew.

Our relationship continued to blossom with more fun dates and growing intimacy. He branched out of his comfort zone by attending yoga classes with me on occasion. To my pleasure, he even accompanied me to see my favorite author, John C. Maxwell, speak at a local college. I was certainly impressed with my new flame. Toby pulled me out of the melancholic stupor I'd been in for months as he urged me with militant advocacy to put my big girl pants on and get my ambition back. All the while, he whimsically swept me off of my feet with romantic surprises and impromptu getaways. I was also highly influenced by his entrepreneurial mindset, which made me start to really think about different ways I could move forward with my life. Truly, the timing of our courtship couldn't have been better. It showed me the stepping stones to take so I could delve into ideas of reshaping my future when I had somewhat lost my way.

Since he owned a successful restaurant in Lima, he was always involved in bettering his business. He frequented conventions, tradeshows, and events that pertained to the restaurant industry, and he was on the board of some local philanthropical committees in Lima as well. Coincidentally, he was also longtime friends with the Elm Tree Pub owners, even though I didn't officially meet him until well after my employment at the pub ended. It was so reassuring to witness all of the tiny dots of my story connect to his at every turn. It never ceases to amaze me how life seems to have a way of revealing the course at its own pace

About five weeks into our unofficial relationship, I accompanied Toby to a food show in Cleveland, Ohio, which was less than three hours away. We made a weekend of it by driving at night on a Friday, and we planned to leave early in the morning on Monday. He booked a room in the same hotel as the convention, so we were able to conveniently settle in for the next three nights. On our first night there, even though we arrived late, we hit up an awesome bar for late-night drinks and delicious grub at a place called the Butcher and the Brewer. It was Toby's idea. It was sweet how thoughtfully he incorporated what he knew about my passions into his diligent schemes. I ordered an in-house distilled honey whiskey mixed with ginger ale and a lemon twist and Toby got a unique and tangy smoked margarita. We shared late night appetizers of BBQ spiced wings, gooey hot spinach and artichoke dip, and delicious carnitas tacos topped with a house-made slaw. He assured me we'd be getting our trendy-bar-foodie-groove on that weekend since he loved to scope the scene of his trade.

In addition to going to the food show, Toby also had an appointment the next day to look at a new oven for his restaurant. This wasn't just any oven; it was a combi oven, which is a combination of a steamer and a convection oven. Toby and I experienced a personal demonstration of the product over a couple-hour period that left us both fascinated and satiated. I was so dazzled by the multifunction capacity of this incredible piece of equipment. It had the capability to control different temperatures and cook times for the food on each individual rack in the oven. With some programming, you can place a variety of food in at the same time and it will cook simultaneously with each rack at its varying degrees. The man presenting the product proved it to us by making steak, fries, asparagus, and mini dessert cakes all at the same time. It was impressive… and delicious. But of course, for all that, it did come with a hefty price tag.

The food show was Sunday. After rolling out of bed at the crack of nine, we made our way down the elevator for the function. The hustle and bustle made the event rather lively. There were people everywhere. Vendors everywhere. Food everywhere! Coffee bars, tea stands, juice makers everywhere. There were rows of meat, seafood, fried food, packaged food, raw food, and a whole entire corner devoted solely to baked goods! It was all free, and it was at my disposal! I was in heaven.

While Toby was looking at some to-go packaging, I meandered over to another live demonstration of a combi oven. And what do ya know? It looked awfully familiar. There were two chefs running the demo: a friendly blond man up on a small stage speaking through his headset microphone while explaining the details of the oven and a beautiful, pin-up-looking girl wearing a chef coat at a table behind him, dishing up something scrumptious.

I walked over to her out of curiosity and asked, "What are you working on over here?"

"These are individual banana pudding desserts," she replied and then continued to describe their composure. "Please help yourself," she insisted.

"Well, don't mind if I do. Thank you!" I said as I grabbed a tiny serving cup from her tray. "Did you make them in the combi oven?"

After only fifteen minutes of conversation and one hell of a banana pudding, this random girl inspired me to take advantage of an opportunity I had never heard of before. Her name was Miranda, and after she explained to me the process she went through to prepare these little bits of heaven, I asked her what her job was. She told me that she was just hired to help out at this food show event but that she was involved in many facets of the food world. She gave me a brief history of her background, including that she was from the Midwest and learned to cook from her grandmother. She told me about different opportunities she had had and how she had been fortunate to make money catering where she lived in St. Louis, Missouri. She also explained that, on the side, she wrote recipes for companies. Then, she told me about a cookbook she wrote called *The Meat Lady* and gave me information on how to look it up.

"Are you a butcher?" I asked.

She was not a butcher by trade, but she had practiced butchery and had learned a great deal about processing animals from her childhood. She informed me about an all-girls butcher retreat she'd attended called Grrls Meat Camp and briefly explained that it was an event where women gather to learn about meat and the art of the butchery.

At the time, I was still wearing a pretty decent splint on my left hand, so it wasn't long into our conversation when Miranda asked me what had happened to my hand.

"I cut my thumb off on a bandsaw," I said, uttering my typical reply.

The conversation played out as it does when other people hear of my injury for the first time: shock, condolences, amazement, and then some connection to a crazy story. Except, with Miranda, she was more curious about what I did for work rather than showing some crazy scar she had obtained. I explained to her I had worked as a meatcutter at a slaughterhouse and how I might be looking for some side income soon. She gave me her contact information and said we could stay in touch about some of the side jobs she was into, like writing recipes and doing food shows, but she also wanted me to look up an upcoming butcher's program to be held in Copenhagen later in the year.

The program was called Butcher's Manifesto. She said that she'd heard about it through Grrls Meat Camp, and she strongly encouraged me to look into it. I was hesitant to jump on the idea at first since my funds were limited and, well, Copenhagen isn't exactly next door, but when she told me they offered a scholarship program and that they pay for some people to attend, I found myself seriously considering it.

"You should write to them about your thumb and see if you could get in," she suggested.

Something about her genuine poise and enthusiasm stuck with me, so I briefly checked out the website and did some basic googling of the topic. At that time, there was not a whole lot of information I could find online, so I decided to put the idea on the back burner and continued to enjoy our weekend getaway in Cleveland.

Toby and I ate and drank our way through local breweries and restaurants—all in the name of research, right?— and he even surprised me with a trip to an awesome, local artisan butcher shop. Since time had passed, I found myself growing more comfortable exposing myself to the butchery world again. I still felt a bit uneasy when I stepped into the butcher shop, but that sickening rush of anxiety was certainly less evident than before. And this time I was with a stout companion who encouraged me to try rekindling my meat love and dive back into my curiosity for comestibles. I didn't want to let my anxiousness stand in the way of this gallant man trying to win my heart.

That trip to Cleveland was inspiring. Toby was a visionary in the restaurant world, and he had worked hard to build his growing business and reputation in Lima. And I felt that drive, his motivation rubbing off on me. He encouraged me to keep dreaming and stay in pursuit of regaining my confidence. He would not let me wallow about my injury. With his support, I diligently started to think of different ways to approach moving onward and upward in my future. And it wasn't long before I gladly acknowledged this man as my boyfriend.

The day after I met my meat angel, Miranda, I took some time to journal in the hotel room.

Cleveland Diaries

<u>April 24, 2017</u>

I am in the midst of new and exciting times. I feel free! I am strong and empowered. I can see myself through a new lens, and I like what I see. I can see the potential before me. I just need to step up to the plate and swing the bat. I may step up and swing time and time again, and I may fail to make a hit over and over, but the truth of the reality is *I will never make a hit from the stands or the sidelines*! I have to keep on keeping on. I have to keep walking up to that plate and taking the risk. But certainly, if I measure the risk by what I am afraid may or may not happen, it's more of an ego issue than it is a danger. Sure, I could suffer tremendous pain from failure, but will I survive? Oh yeah. And guess what? It's likely that I will grow stronger and wiser and become more empowered, expanding my horizons exponentially from the potential failure. And on the flip side, if I gain success or achieve what I set out to do, I will experience growth. I will gain momentum, set newer and bigger goals, and meet new people. By walking through doors of opportunity, one can perhaps suddenly be exposed to worlds of different experiences and advances.

As I sit here in this hotel room, I can't help but allow my imagination to tread down the likeness of what I want. Yesterday, I was supplied with a familiar taste of a vision that once lived in my heart, and today, I am blessed with time to reflect on how I can continue to grow my dreams and ideas. I know adventure awaits around mysterious corners, and I cannot wait to embrace it and unleash the ideas of what could be.

Butcher's Manifesto

As far as my recovery was going, I was in an unknown place physically, mentally, and emotionally. Summer was near, and I had just had my second surgery. This was a short operation where the doctor removed a stabilizing pin in my thumb that was initially placed to hold together my reconstructed metacarpophalangeal joint. The pin was ready to come out—literally. After bumping my hand on a doorframe by accident, the metal started to protrude under my skin. In a fit of agony, I called the doctor's nurse, and she told me to come in immediately. Once the doc examined my thumb, he scheduled surgery for two days later. He encouraged me that if it pierced through the skin before I was due to come in on Wednesday to just go ahead and yank it out. Was that a joke? Nope.

That procedure really was no big deal. It was mid-May, some six months after my initial injury, and my doctor projected I probably wouldn't be fit to return to work until July—another six weeks. I was thankful for his caution and care while I was on medical leave, since pretty much every step of the process depended on my surgeon's medical opinion. Since he'd been in the game for decades, and my thumb was astonishingly reattached with precision, I trusted and heeded his every word. He told me that once he deemed me medically stable, I should pursue the option of vocational rehabilitation offered by the insurance company. However, he did not recommend that I return to butchery due to the long-term effects that would eventually diminish my thumb's overall health.

My life at the time was a two-step boogie between me and the DWC. The DWC was short for the Ohio

Division of Workers' Compensation, an insurance program designed to offer compensation and medical benefits to employees who were injured on the job in exchange for the injured worker to not sue the employer for those benefits. Typically, an employer will pay a monthly or annual fee to cover their business, and if a claim is filed, then the employer does not have to deal directly with making decisions in the claim. It can be a lengthy, pricey process as well, especially for a catastrophic claim like mine. Thankfully the company also offered psychological support in the event of trauma. This program allowed me to receive the foundation of much needed mental healthcare throughout my recovery as well. I was in constant, direct contact with my various case managers throughout my claim. With each revelation of the psychologist's and surgeon's notes, I'd elevate through the system's channels and become closer to the end of the line, where I could return to work and no longer depend on the assistance from the insurance company and its many facets.

A couple of long, drawn-out weeks later, the thought of the Butcher's Manifesto came across my mind again. This time, I was less distracted and rather bored in my room one night, so I began to look into the program. I discovered there would be a gathering in Copenhagen of fifty butchers later that summer. I also spent a little more time looking into the scholarship program and researching the logistics of possibly getting to Denmark to attend this unusual meat retreat.

I guess I was thankful for the ongoing delays with my thumb's healing because it led me to get the report of "six more weeks" once again at the end of June. This meant the timing of the Butcher's Manifesto could potentially work out because I would be released to return to work right before the retreat. I would be medically free to travel and knuckle down, but I wouldn't be tied to a job or need to ask for time off. However, the thought of pursuing this European butchers' convention did cause some trepidation for a while. I thought, with my limited resources, restricted income, and the constant uncertainty of my living situation, that it wouldn't be wise to take a trip overseas, even though it called to me like a lighthouse calls to a ship on a dark and stormy night.

Ever since I cut my thumb off, I was bashful about my situation. I had followed my curious heart across the country to stay on a farm in the middle of nowhere to live and work with people who were strangers at first. Somehow, I ended up working at a slaughterhouse and found myself fond of fondling meat. Then, I lost a limb (for a day) in the process. Where the hell could my life go from there? At some point, I had lost the vivacious passion for meat processing, but deep within me, my love for food and the industry remained. My infatuation now was with the greater understanding of where food comes from and how it gets from point A to B. Many times in my life, I preferred to cut out the middleman so that I could better understand the processes of receiving things I want (which in this case was fresh, tasty meat) as well as become more resourceful, more self-sufficient or self-sustaining.

So, thanks to my meat-induced interests, the serendipitous meeting with Miranda, and the boatload of free time from being on medical leave for many months, I decided to attempt to attend this Butcher's Manifesto. I used my knack for storytelling, and I sent an email application along with a somewhat endearing story of a bloody butcher scar. I wanted so badly to participate in this experience, obtain further education on the subject, and prove not only to the naysayers who said I would never cut meat again but also to myself that, even though I'd been

202

through trauma and painful setbacks, I could still pursue the dreams within my heart that were unsettled.

I received an invitation to join the conference in August of 2017. It was a three-day endeavor with housing and food provided by the organization. When I opened the email that invited me to fly across the pond, I was floored. There had been something inside me that told me I was meant to go, but when I actually read the welcoming words, I couldn't believe it.

My family went back and forth on supporting me on the matter, but every time I looked into my heart, all signs pointed to yes. I'll admit, however, there was a time where I seriously entertained not going, mainly because my doctor had recommended I not go back into the industry due to the high risk for early arthritis, the severe pain I felt from my thumb's cold intolerance, and the lack of strength in my left hand. So, I was left weighing my outcomes on the risk versus reward scale. These truths really would come into account if I were to stand in a cold processing room all day, repetitively grasping and cutting meat. It just wouldn't work out well for my long-term hand health. But the reward of expanding my horizons and trying my hand at something that beckoned me ended up outweighing the risks. So one day, I just woke up and bought a ticket to Copenhagen.

Of course, it wouldn't be *my* story if I didn't have some other ingredients in the mix. Once again, my uncle flew me from Ohio to Florida for the family reunion in the beginning of August. Knowing I wouldn't be the same ocean-slayer I'd been in previous years, all of my relatives encouraged me to come down for some R and R and much needed family time. As an extra treat, both my boyfriend Toby and my friend Charlotte from Nevada flew into the Keys for a few days as well, which turned out to be the perfect recipe for a relishable vacation for all. It also just so happened that when I opted to go to Denmark, I bought my round-trip ticket to fly out and back from Florida.

I had some odds stacked against me though, and my resources were dwindling, but I didn't care. My heart was excited that my dreams would be pursued as long as blood ran through my veins. I had no idea what I was in for, but it had always been a dream of mine to go to Europe, so I was really killing a couple birds with one stone here. Little did I know my life would once again be forever changed. Little did I know that all of the scrambled pieces of the puzzle I'd been fighting to place would come together in a brief stint overseas.

I was nervous to leave the country by myself, but I was excited to meet like-minded people and have an adventure! I boarded the plane with just a small carry-on crammed with work clothes, toiletries, a book, and my journal. I'd only be going for a quick five days, of which included nearly two days of travel. Most everyone attending the conference would be staying at the Folkets Madhus, translated as "the people's food house," where the event was taking place.

When I landed in Denmark, I was met with pleasure when I learned that most people spoke English. I meandered through the airport to find the ticket counter where I would receive instructions to take the metro to the City Centre. From there, I hopped on a bus that would drop me a short five-minute walk to the venue. While getting off the bus, I noticed a few other potential butchers, and I zealously inquired if they were part of the Butcher's Manifesto. They were, and the smiles radiated between the four of us as we made our way along the sidewalk that wonderful afternoon. One girl was from New Orleans, and the two guys hailed from Germany and Austria, respectively, although the man who lived in

Vienna was originally from the States. We strolled through a chain-link gate that surrounded the industrial-looking area. After a few more steps, a huge black sign with bold white letters that read Folkets Madhus was in sight. We had made it!

We were greeted by a friendly brunette woman, and she informed us that we were of the first to arrive. After a brief exchange with the few people working the event, we were checked in. She escorted us to our living quarters for the next few nights, which turned out to be an indoor soccer field building across from the Folkets Madhus. There were dozens of bright yellow tents set up on a few of the synthetic courts, complete with sleeping bags and pads. To some, it may not have seemed to be luxurious, but for me, it was beyond perfect. I took a few minutes to settle in and write in my journal in order to capture and express the heightened emotions raging through me. I couldn't stop smiling. I was eager to see what more was in store.

For the welcome dinner, a mostly whole hog was mounted on a rotating spit and stuffed with lamb. The meat was slow cooked for hours over a bed of hot coals carefully tended to by the various hosts. Paired with an array of barbequed vegetables and a seemingly endless tap of beer, the feast was certainly fit for a band of butchers. Attendees from all of the world arrived in various intervals throughout the evening. We gathered around the provisions and exchanged friendly greetings and lighthearted conversations about our travels, families and various professions. Let the networking begin! While we ate, the founders of Butcher's Manifesto informed us that the weekend would be jam-packed with workshops, education and activities, including participating in the Copenhagen Cooking and Food Festival that Sunday. Our group was due to participate in the annual festival by showcasing some of the facets of our industry. We came together to represent our craft to the public through various approaches like 'Meet a Butcher' conversations, offering a variety of freshly grilled cuts of meat, a whole carcass breakdown demonstration, and appealing interactive art installations. The weekend was filled with high energy and enthusiasm, information and enlightenment, community and connection. Although we were basically strangers at first, we formed an impressive bond that weekend and it was an overall accomplishment!

Not only did I meet butchers, chefs, and restauranteurs during the short-lived trip to Denmark, but I also came to realize there were more facets to the meat world than I had been aware of, including meat intellectuals, advocates, and authors who actually helped found this specific organization. All across the globe, people were fighting to keep the craft and age-old traditions alive. For three days, there were nonstop discussions about needs, challenges, and potential solutions for this cornerstone industry.

The convention itself was only three days long, but when I bought my airline ticket, I had decided to stay an extra day in Denmark in hopes of doing some exploring. Instead of gallivanting around Copenhagen on Tuesday, I was presented with the opportunity to stick around the Folkets Madhus and help out with the next event being hosted. That endeavor was a gathering of multigenerational German butchers named the Truffeljagd, translated as the "truffle hunt." However, despite the name, the group focused on keeping the craft and German butcher traditions alive. Their event purposefully overlapped with Butcher's Manifesto in hopes that even more connections could be made within the trade. Very few of those German butchers spoke English; therefore, it proved to be difficult for me to speak with most of them.

An American traveling educator of the craft, Adam Danforth, was leading a workshop for the German butchers about breaking down a carcass in order to inspire conversation and connection among the attendees. He demonstrated the breakdown of a goat as the Germans intently watched. I gladly contributed my willing hands by helping to cook and serve the different cuts to the onlookers as they talked about the various textures and tastes. Then, three more carcasses were introduced so the Germans could team up and show each other different techniques and traditions practiced in their hometown shops.

It was quite impressive to watch the many hands gather and work together to perform the whole animal butchery. Pretty much every conversation in the room was in German, so I just watched in awe of their skills. One man in particular, Hans Heindl, blew my mind with his abilities. It was obvious he was incredibly gifted in his art. I observed his six-inch blade dance with the anatomy of the goat, effortlessly pulling out perfect cuts of meat while the bones were left almost spotless. I had never seen such craftsmanship before my very eyes. He produced flawless cuts of meat with the swipes of his knife, never using a bandsaw.

"Will you tell him it's an honor to watch him work?" I leaned over and asked the blond, middle-aged woman who served as the group's translator.

After exchanging some words with her in German, the stalwart man looked at me with a smile and said, "Danke schoen."

"I would love to learn to butcher like that," I said to her, not knowing she would then reiterate the words to him.

After another brief conversation with Hans, the translator turned to me and said, "He said you are welcome to learn from him. He would be happy to teach you."

"Wow. Thank you," I said, shaking his hand. I didn't think it would actually happen, but I was unaware of what a single handshake meant in the German culture.

A short time later, I found myself speaking with the translator and a thirty-something German woman about the impressive skills of Hans. The translator told me this woman was the daughter of Hans. I grew excited to compliment her father, and the translator helped us to have a conversation about their butchery in Southern Germany, an area commonly known as Bavaria. The daughter's name was Carmen, and I learned the family owned seven small butcheries in Bavaria.

I told her what a privilege it was to watch her father, and I again said how great it would be to learn from him. She explained that it was common for butchers to have apprentices and it would not be a problem to host me for a time if I was so inclined. We both grew in excitement, although it was difficult to express with words. Luckily, body language and facial expressions are universal. We exchanged information, and Carmen explained that they had living quarters where I could stay, that their company could pay me to work and learn, and that I could even bring my dogs.

I was baffled. What just happened? I had just received another invitation to move somewhere completely foreign to me where I could live and work with strangers in order to further my education for my once-beloved practice. This sounded awfully familiar…

When I returned home, I posted to Facebook:

A network is defined by the English Oxford Dictionary as an arrangement of intersecting horizontal and vertical lines; a group or system of interconnected people or things. And success is defined as the accomplishment of an aim or purpose.

This weekend, Butcher's Manifesto successfully created a network of like-minded individuals who possess essential and complementary functions to the grand operation of the meat industry.

This is just the beginning! I am so honored, excited, and ready to team up with some extraordinary people who are part of the food revolution!

With courage, dedication, education, outreach, communication, action, and patience, I believe, together, we will positively influence our market and create sustainable change that will benefit all parties involved from "farm to fork."

Get ready, world! We're a bunch of meat-crazy bastards, and our flames have been lit!

In the following weeks after returning home from the Butcher's Manifesto, I stayed in touch with Carmen. We exchanged emails about possibilities and timelines of me potentially coming to Germany. She would write to me in German, and I would copy and paste the conversation into Google Translate. She would do the same with my English emails. We jokingly said we should teach each other our native languages, but mostly, we relied on technology to communicate.

Meanwhile, back in Ohio, my circumstances once again changed, and the excitement from my European meat retreat began to fade. It's crazy how quickly the plummet comes after the peak.

Tate

As it played out, it wasn't until I returned from this meat-scursion that my doctor deemed me medically stable, so when I returned to Ohio, I began to jump through the hoops of returning to work. I had a case supervisor assigned to work with me to help me transition from being on medical leave to enrolling in a vocational rehabilitation program. This was the next stage of my journey. For those who receive workers' comp, if you are not returning to the same job due to injury, they offer to retrain you for another career. This involves being assessed and taking tests to help with job placement. The case supervisor then assists with finding a new employer. The DWC will offer compensation until training is complete and returning to work has been achieved.

I got the ball rolling in Ohio and followed the timely steps it took to get into vocational rehab. Since I was now medically stable, my monetary medical leave benefits ended; however, once I was active in the vocational rehab program, I was assured I would receive some income during the retraining phase, and then once employed, unless eligible, I would no longer receive financial aid from the DWC.

At the time, it seemed like the right move to make. I still suffered great pain in my left hand and had ridiculous cold intolerance. Just the slight touch of a cold object would send sharp pains up my entire left arm. So, for the time being, returning to butchery was out, even though my recent trip opened my eyes to other potential possibilities for my future. But as far as finding immediate means for employment, I knew returning to work at a bar or restaurant would be difficult as well due to the pretty high demands of having two functioning hands, which left door number three: vocational rehab.

I was actually excited for this new, door-opening endeavor. In my eyes, the sky was the limit, and I had hoped this tool would help to get me on track for a new career, especially since I wasn't one of those people who had a deep passion for any particular job, but more of a general displacement for labor that aligned my aspirations.

Well, let's just say my excitement for vocational rehab wore off quickly when the results of the four-hour test I had taken left me with three not-so-attractive career options. Apparently, I qualified to be a funeral assistant, an escort, and a parlor chaperone.

You've got to be kidding me, I thought when I read the results in an email. "What the heck is a parlor chaperone? And an escort? Come on!" I whined to myself in disbelief.

This was exact point in time when I started to lose faith in this program. *All of that testing and all of the "possibility," and* this *is what my test results told me? Lord, help me,* I thought.

Just a few days after I arrived home from Europe, I met up with my friend Joe, who I had originally met during my time as a bartender at the pub. We developed an acquaintanceship when we first met, but it wasn't until we bumped into each other at a Verizon store earlier that summer that we reconnected and eventually became dear friends. I hardly recognized him when I ran into him because, since I'd last seen him, he had been diagnosed with a disease called alopecia that resulted in the loss of all of his facial and body hair. The Joe I knew was fully bearded with curly brown hair and bushy eyebrows. He explained to me the trauma of his diagnosis during our timely conversation that day, and of course, I shared with him all I'd been through in the past year as well. We connected over the similarities of emotions we experienced on our individual journeys. We exchanged phone numbers and stayed in touch pretty regularly from then on.

He came out to the farm to hear all about my summer stories, and we took my dogs out for a day of exploring in the woods. It was during this leisurely day that my dog, Tato, obtained an injury to her spinal cord. By the next day, it was clear to me that she was hurt, but it wasn't until a couple days later that she could no longer use her hind legs. She'd often play hard and swim literally for hours in the pond, so it wasn't uncommon for her to be sore and laid up after wearing herself out. This time though, I could tell something was definitely wrong. It was early in the morning on a Sunday when I decided to take her to a nearby veterinarian's office that was open and took walk-ins. They examined her for all of fifteen minutes and encouraged me to take her directly to the emergency vet about an hour away. They said something was clearly wrong with her nervous system, but they didn't have the advanced acute technology that the other place had. I felt their compassion for my hurting pup when they didn't charge me anything for their professional opinion that day. I think the doctor knew I'd be spending quite a bit of money on diagnosing her problem.

I waited for roughly six hours in the lobby at the emergency vet, and it took about ninety minutes for them to take Tato back for the initial physical exam. My heart hurt for her while my mind pondered and feared the worst. Due to their recommendations, I opted to get her some X-rays and a blood analysis, which was an expensive ordeal in itself. The results of the blood tests were negative, meaning they didn't detect any irregularities in her hormones or organs. However, the X-rays revealed that it was possible that pressure from one of the vertebrates on Tato's spinal cord may have been what caused her to lose function in her hind legs. They informed me that they couldn't accurately diagnose the problem without performing an MRI. They explained the steps of trial and error treatment that involved a routine dose of pain-relievers and steroids, and no movement for a week to six-months, depending on the extent of the injury. The treatment plan I opted for had us back for a follow-up appointment in two weeks. Once we determined if she did or did not make progress, I could opt for an MRI, which would cost around two thousand dollars. I was heartbroken by the situation but determined to do everything in my power to see her be able to swim again.

I was so sad to see my little buttercup in this situation. She was my rock-solid support, my partner in crime, my little baby Tate. She was a Pitbull, eleven years old at the time, and weighed in at a solid thirty-three pounds. I got Tato from an old boss at the Tamarack who lived in an apartment and could not keep up with the energy the little pitty had. At the time, I lived in a house with a yard with Jack, so we didn't hesitate to bring her into our family when I was only nineteen years old. She had truly been by my side through so many milestones in my life: break-ups, cross-country feats, and everything in between. Hell, I planned many hours and adventures of that decade solely around her love for water. And boy, did she love water! She pined for any kind of water, be it lakes, rivers, creeks, streams, pools, buckets, mud puddles, hoses, and more. She would bark and play and splash around any body of liquid she could find. Oftentimes, if we neared a source of water while riding in the car, she would begin to pant heavily in excitement. I think she could smell it. She would even happily go paddle boarding with me; she would intermittently ride on the board for a little and then jump off to swim alongside me before doing it all over, time and time again.

After a few days on the steroids, it seemed like she was making progress, but in reality, the injury was just being masked by the medicine. After another week of enduring the restless nights of carrying her up and down the stairs to urinate frequently—thanks to the steroids—we went back in for our follow-up appointment. The staff advised me to consider the MRI, which could possibly lead to another three-thousand-dollar procedure, depending on the results. I told them I needed some time to weigh my options. They gave me plenty of information and explained to me different scenarios for her situation, telling me if I wanted to schedule the procedure that I could cancel it at any time, even the day of, but it would be in my best interest to make the appointment. I obliged and took my girl home for a snuggle session. We slept curled up together on the porch so if she had to go outside, I didn't have to carry her up and down the stairs.

She'd been suffering without advancement for two days straight, so I attempted to MacGyver a sling out of a scarf to assist me in assisting her to relieve herself when we were on the lawn. She was already timid when she had to do her business, so the empathy I felt for her having to somewhat schedule her duties only broke my heart more. To my almost surprise, the sling actually had a greater affect than just alleviating my discomfort, and by the next morning, she was able to take four or five steps on her own with the pressure of the sling holding her hips high. She certainly still struggled to pee, but I was amazed to see her take those staggering steps. Over the phone, I shared my concerns with my wise friend Taylor from back home, who used to work for a vet, and she encouraged me to get a second opinion before getting an MRI and to make sure to get her urine sampled. I took her to a different vet to see what they had to say. Lo and behold, Tato also had a mild bladder infection, and with a dose of antibiotics, she clearly experienced some relief in her ability to pee. Her slight sense of progress warmed my spirits.

I cancelled the MRI appointment due to the recent improvements and figured I could wait another week or two to see what more might develop. Every day, she got incrementally better. I kept her in her kennel in my bedroom with a rotation of towels to protect the floor from the unexpected and inadvertent messes. She was rather content being tucked away in my room amidst her difficult situation. She inspired me with her resilience and perseverance. I spent much of my time laying on the floor with her, rubbing her belly and trying to keep my other dog, Bugsy, a slightly obnoxious Boston Terrier, from disturbing her peace.

Two more weeks went by, and her progress hit a plateau. By this time, it was late-September, and I was caught between caring for my laid-up pup and going through the motions of getting into vocational rehab. While I was running here and there to pursue furthering my ambitions of being a potential funeral assistant (kidding), I couldn't stop thinking about my Tato princess and the dire dysphoria I felt for what the truths were of my entire situation. By then, I had no income. I was still in the beginning "assessment phase" for vocational rehab, and since I was not yet officially enrolled, I wasn't yet eligible for financial support. I couldn't pursue other legitimate means for work if I wanted to be in the program. I struggled as it were to adjust to the physical and emotional weakened state of having experienced that regrettable trauma. If I didn't have my kind and generous adopted grandparents at the time, I would have literally had nothing.

I still had regrets and anxiety from my own injury. I still felt the need to prove something to myself. *I am tough. I have to be tough. I need to be strong and brave and bold. I need to keep fighting. I can't let these circumstances get the best of me. I cannot be defeated.*

If dealing with all of this wasn't bad enough, most of my Ohio family and friends, unfortunately, told me that I should consider putting my dog down. This was certainly not what I wanted to hear, and in my opinion, she was making progress. Despite what others thought was best, I knew my little Potato, and she was recovering—slowly, but surely. We were two tough gals, and we were going to recover together, even if it took us awhile.

One night, Toby invited me over for dinner with some of his family who was visiting from out of town. I had met them before when we traveled to Virginia Beach for a last-minute trip over Father's Day weekend. We had such a great time in their hometown that summer, so I looked forward to seeing them again. They encouraged me to bring my dogs with me, and Toby helped me set Tato up in her kennel on his porch. The teenagers gave her heaps of attention and pets, and I was able to actually relax for a bit and enjoy the evening. We dined on some lobsters that Toby and I brought back from the Keys. But it wasn't long before Tato made a stinky mess in her kennel. I was slightly embarrassed and imagined it would be stressful for both Tato and I if we stayed, so I said my goodbyes and loaded the pups up to head back to the farm. I was an emotional wreck when I pulled away from his house. It was late, and I was beginning to lose hope for Tato's healing.

Once again, I found myself on the side of the road, bawling uncontrollably and wondering what I could do and where I could go. I decided to call my mom, and before I knew it, I was hysterically confessing that I was not ready to put her down, but I was at the end of my capacity to handle this on my own.

"Mom," I sobbed.

"Honey, it's okay. Just breathe." Her voice was instantly calming.

"Mom, she's still in so much pain. She can't go to the bathroom on her own, and everyone says I should put her down," I cried.

"Is there anywhere you can go right now? I don't think you should be alone."

"I don't know. It's late, and I have the dogs, and Toby has family in town…" I searched my mind for answers, for hope.

"Honey, I think it's time for you to come home." Her words sunk straight into my heart. "Just try to calm down tonight. We'll figure something out, but right now, just focus on getting somewhere safe. I love you. Everything is going to be okay."

After getting my bearings, I called Cindy for refuge. She invited me to come over with my sick pup and stated she would take care of us. I drove to her house, and she quickly took over the caretaker role for both Tato and me that night. I was utterly exhausted, but I was wound tight.

Relieved, I curled up next Tato on the floor of Cindy's study.

She said in her motherly tone, "Kris, you don't have to put her down if you don't want to. You know what's best for her."

It was as if she had sprinkled her fairy godmother dust on me, momentarily releasing me of my current stress and the burden of reality. I was no longer sleeping on the floor by my sick dog, facing a difficult decision. I was in a safe haven.

We slept—hard.

The next morning, Cindy took Tato out to her lawn and put her in the sunshine on the grass. When I woke up and came outside, I saw that happy smile and gentle wag of her tail, and I knew it wasn't over for her.

She had just needed more time and support. It's crazy how a night of deep sleep can change things.

I realized that was exactly what I needed too. I decided that day, on the drive back to the farm, that I needed to move home. I knew my family in Reno would help me in all the right ways. I wasn't ready to give up either, not on Tato, not on myself, and Ohio just couldn't give me what I needed anymore.

I ran my decision by my inner circle, both in Ohio and back home, and all I received was the encouragement to do what I felt was best. I've always had a keen understanding of my internal compass, and I knew Reno was where it was pointing.

Within three weeks, my mom was on a one-way flight to Ohio, prepared to drive back across the country to Nevada to bring her baby girl and grandpups home.

Goodbye

Amidst the decision to move home, my case supervisor informed me that, thankfully, I could still receive the same vocational rehab in Nevada. She explained the process might take some time to get me established in Reno, as I would need to find a company who would get Ohio certified to rehabilitate me for work. She gave me tips on how to navigate the transition and wished me and my dog the best in our future.

I had a follow-up appointment scheduled with my surgeon for October 19, 2018. Therefore, we planned to leave Friday, October 20, to head back to Nevada. I got all of my affairs in order and even found a company willing to take me in Reno for the insurance program. Things were falling into place, and my Ohio adventure was nearing its end.

I spent the weeks prior to my doctor's appointment packing my things and saying my goodbyes. It was a bittersweet time in my journey because I didn't wholeheartedly want to leave Ohio. I loved it there, and for a while, I had been determined to stick it out and prove to myself this injury wouldn't defeat me. But in reality, I had more than myself to think about, and my love for Tato pushed me to make my decision. In my heart, I thought if it was the end of her days, I wanted her to spend those days at home. Nevertheless, I knew in the pit of my gut that saying goodbye would be painfully difficult.

I shared fond farewell hugs with everyone: the farmers, the steakhouse crew, the slaughterhouse family, the pubgoers, the physical therapists, and even the bowlers. I brought Carl from the bowling alley a goodbye cupcake just to make sure I got the last word. He wasn't there the day I dropped it off, but I heard later that he got it and ate it. Only in my imagination do I picture him smiling, though he probably wasn't. When I told Toby of my decision, he hinted that he kind of assumed it would happen. He empathized for me, and he'd come to love Tato to an extent as well, so I think he understood the situation. We had an excellent run at our relationship, but I certainly needed more than he could give me at the time, so we ended our love affair on a high note. He offered to make the haul to Nevada with me, but by that point, I just wanted my mom. We decided to keep seeing each other until my departure. We still cared about each other; our timing just wasn't right. We soaked in those last few weeks before I left, doing all the things we had loved to do and trying to squeeze in a few new adventures too.

It was hard to say goodbye to Toby, don't get me wrong, but the goodbye that caught me off guard was Juke's. Even though we didn't love each other like we once did, we loved each other like I'd never known before. He was such an adult about things. He carried no hard feelings or adolescent reactions to the many twists in our relationship, and no matter what, he always showed up. He held space for me in his world, and he showed me friendship and understanding like none other. He even built a portable dog-sized set of stairs as a going-away gift to help Tato get on the bed when she was back home and feeling better. This gesture fed my hope that everything was going to be okay, that I still had more time with Tato. Juke. Thoughtful, mature Juke. From the very beginning, Juke had made the effort. He had been all the things I needed him to be at all the right times. Yeah, this goodbye was one of the hardest.

I slowly packed up all of my belongings and relived the fond memories as I touched the physical evidence of many memories made. I didn't want to bother anyone to help me pack, but my pal Joe knew that I could use a hand, so he came out to the farm to help me load my big furniture items into my trailer. He was in tune with his emotional side and served as a stand-up buddy to keep me focused and supported during this difficult transition. Once my room was empty, the reality sunk in. This was the end. I had thought it was the end many times before, but this was actually it. I was leaving, starting a new chapter in an old place.

Most of my girlfriends took the time to send me off with warm wishes and conversations that ended with, "I can't wait to see you again." Most of them shared with me their own stories of crossroads, endings, and beginnings. I felt a sense of peace about where I was on my journey and a conviction in my decisions. It was still hard to really express my gratitude and appreciation to each and every one of them. How did I get so lucky to have so many dear souls care about me and love me? With each goodbye, I felt empowered and optimistic for the next chapter in my story. I was ready to move on to the next phase of my recovery. I had finally accepted the fact that my limitations and pain were just things I would have to live with. I felt like I was turning a corner, and I was beginning to get excited about moving home and having a fresh start there.

The day before I left Ohio, I saw my doctor for a farewell check-up. I had anticipated tear-filled goodbyes and heartfelt thank yous during that office visit. Instead, within just a few minutes of examining my thumb and listening to my painful complaints, he informed my mother and me that I could greatly benefit from another surgery due to the terrible cold intolerance I was experiencing.

"Your capillary refill in your thumb is lagging. The pain you experience is likely a result of your nerve endings that can cause hypersensitivity. Some people have this sort of reaction to the hardware in their body as well. With surgery, we could reduce your pain anywhere from 15 to 50 percent."

We were leaving the next day. My things were packed. My mom had purchased a one-way ticket so she could drive with me back across the country. Even still, she asked the doctor, "When could you do this surgery?"

"Well, workers' comp will have to approve the surgery, and first, they have to approve the diagnosis, so pending their authorizations, I imagine it will be just after the first of the year," Dr. Wozniak replied. He briefly explained how the process would go.

"Oh, this is great news, honey! A 15 to 50 percent decrease in your pain is huge!" my mother reassured me.

Although I trusted my doctor, probably more than anyone else on the planet at that time, I was disheartened by the fact that I was not at the end of this road. However, the confidence my doctor exuded for a better end result allowed me to have some excitement. He had impressed everyone with my thumb's remarkable function up until that point, so I knew following his advice would be the best direction to go. He gave me assurance that the wheels would be in motion with workers' comp for the authorizations. He encouraged me to come back to Ohio for the surgery so he could see his work through to the end, reemphasizing that the results would be worth it.

Having to continue on this pursuit for the best recovery possible wasn't so simple. I wanted so badly to be done with the medical side of this process so I could focus on getting my life back on track, but the long-term needs of having a fully functioning thumb took precedence over the immediate desire to put it behind me. Although I was headed home, Ohio just wasn't done with me yet.

Due to the doctor's notes from that visit, I was informed that I was no longer eligible for vocational rehab because another potential surgery loomed.

"If you're going to have another surgery, we cannot retrain you for work. We must know that you are medically stable and that your physical limitations are in order for us to follow the workers' comp guidelines to get you back to work," my case supervisor informed me.

"So what do I do next?" I asked.

"Well, once he schedules the surgery, you can receive medical benefits again, and then after surgery, we can start this process over. Since you already did most of the testing, it should go a little faster next time," she said, ensuring I understood the process.

The doctor's office told me that the doctor first needed to diagnose me with the problem that he could then surgically treat. The DWC would then have to approve the diagnosis and then approve the surgery, and these actions take time. I was told it would still be another month or so until the DWC could approve the medical advancements for my case because the case needed to be reviewed by a third-party physician. It was a waiting game, and luckily, I had plenty of distractions to keep me occupied during this time.

In the meanwhile, we made the journey home. It seemed like a hop, skip, and a jump now that I was a seasoned missioner. My mom tended to Tato throughout our drive and gave her all the lovin's she needed while I steadfastly stayed at the wheel. We made the drive in three long days—nearly record time. Once we arrived in sight of the glorious mountains that I loved so much, I knew it wouldn't be long until I was home sweet home. It was time, once again, to start over.

Although I did not have an income, I had incredible support from family and friends who helped me to stay afloat. Since I lived back at home with my brother, he generously heeded the role of the breadwinner in our household for a while. I worked a few odd jobs, babysat for friends and family, and I also sold a few of my possessions for extra cash. I focused on enjoying the holiday season, taking care of Tato, and adjusting to being back in my place of origin. I was happy and excited for the relief of having my support system near me. And Tato continued to make progress, eventually no longer needing her sling. We even caught her trying to climb the stairs within just a few weeks of being home. These glorious truths reassured me that I had made the right move.

Of course, I still checked the status of my insurance claim daily. With zero forward movement on my case, I found myself falling down the slippery slope of depression. I felt helpless and lost trying to navigate a path of which I had little understanding and even less control. More often than not, I just wanted to shut down emotionally. I began to feel like I was no longer receiving help, guidance, or support from this once hopeful process. The waiting really was the hardest part.

"This is exactly why people hire lawyers," a friend told me. "Because lawyers study the law, and they understand all of the ins and outs and hoops to jump through."

I felt even more like a helpless victim when I heard these statements, but I knew they were true. Just when I was beginning to accept my situation, to feel ready to go down the path before me in the direction of vocational rehabilitation, it came to an abrupt halt, and I was left waiting for something to give. Without income and with little communication from the DWC, I felt like I was stuck in a waiting room. I was waiting for guidance. Waiting for help. Waiting for someone to make a decision. Working with that insurance company was a test of my patience, to say the least. I became no stranger to the headaches, anxiety, and frustration that came with the territory. The DWC was, for a time, a pinnacle part of my story. But that slowly changed. The whole process was an emotional roller coaster. It was a lot of effort and a drawn-out pain in the ass to deal with adjusters and convince case managers that I wasn't faking an amputation. Oftentimes, injured individuals can be whiney, manipulative, and sometimes false victims who feel entitled to compensation, support, and aid for their work-related ailments, so I understood the maddening effect it could have on those working on the other end of the telephone. But that wasn't me. Although I am grateful to have received the support from the system that I did, I certainly had to endure some agonizing times, and I almost lost hope in the process. But even amidst the looming depression, there was something about being home that encouraged me to keep trying, like my inner drive had been sparked again, and I knew I couldn't give up.

I must call. I must bug. I must be the squeaky wheel! I thought. I sat in front of my computer, staring at the "pending" status of the aforementioned diagnosis of my claim. "I've learned this truth before, and here I am needing to practice it again. So it's time to pick yourself up and move forward. Do not shut down," I said out loud. "Reach out to those who love you and support you and ask them for help! There are people around you who are willing to help you, but you must ask for it. Most people want to help. Just figure out what you need help with and ask!"

I decided that, come Monday morning, I would make calls and ask questions and, well, squeak! I needed to stop feeling bad for myself and take action. I knew I would eventually gain some momentum if I just kept trying.

I finally hit a tipping point when my case manager said, "This system wasn't designed and catered to Karissa Block." It kind of hurt my feelings to hear her be so crass, but in hindsight, and after talking with my parents about it, I understood she was just doing her nine-to-five job, and sometimes that meant giving the harsh truth.

After that phone call was the exact moment when I decided to hire a lawyer. I didn't know what else to do, and both of my parents advised me that it was the right move to make when dealing with an insurance claim of that stature. When I was in the hospital immediately following the accident, my boss at Smith and Wollensky had given me the phone number of one of his friends who worked as a workers' comp attorney. The lawyer gave me some advice here and there over the phone, but never pressured me to retain him. He was professional, cordial, and filled with the knowledge of the law. Some thirteen months later, I finally reached out and officially hired him to represent me.

I was initially labeled as "disabled" because of my injury. I guess amputating a digit and having it replanted qualifies you as one who isn't able to perform at the same capacity as prior to the injury. However, I did not want to use the injury as a crutch. I was not looking for handouts or support any further than what the doctor ordered. In fact, my mother had to take charge of the situation before I was even released from the hospital because I was in denial about how bad my injury was and how long my recovery would take. Little did I know, it would be some fifteen months before I even returned to work… and another four after that until I would be fully medically released.

I had gotten into some heated arguments with some folks about the process of workers' comp and how many people abuse the system. I know that does happen,

226

but I'm sure, given the situation, anyone would appreciate what the system has to offer if they needed it to use it. In fact, I found the DWC to be a blessing in my life. It was hard for me to accept at first that I needed help, especially since I was determined to overcome this mess and go back to work as soon as possible. But in reality, I qualified for aid because I *needed* it, and it took me some time to realize the fear of accepting that I had been a victim of a terrible accident was hindering me. I had always been pretty self-reliant, but I quickly learned that there was no shame in using tools that are put in place to help individuals through transitional times. And I was certainly smack-dab in the midst of transition.

PTSD

It's hard to write about overcoming adversity when you haven't overcome it. I'd rather lie in bed and ignore the day, distract myself with Netflix, or get high. My most recent psychologist, Dr. T, calls me out on my avoidance tactics. He reassures me that it's common for those who suffer from post-traumatic stress disorder, but he also tells me that it doesn't work to rid the fears, anxieties, and overwhelming memories of the traumatic images that are stained in my brain. They're bound to come back if I keep ignoring them.

I remember them creeping up on me one morning in the shower. The hot water raised my body temperature, and I let it sting as the blood cells in my body slowly started to come alive within me. A mere flash of the vivid recollection of a thumb on the dark, gray cement appeared in the corner of my eye.

Fuck.

Hysteria consumed me, and I lost my balance immediately. I fell down, almost fainting, but caught myself on the edges of the tub. I sobbed instantaneously and uncontrollably for what seemed like an hour.

I looked down at my hand. I cried because of what I had lost. And then I cried harder because of what I still have. I have my thumb. It's beautiful. And it works. And I'm okay.

You made a mistake. You weren't paying attention. This is your fault, and now you are suffering the consequences. The familiar words echoed from me to myself as I tried to justify the anger and frustration I felt while the porcelain tub embraced me ever so gently.

"Karissa, accidents happen. That's why they are called accidents," Dr. T stated after I had explained my spell in the shower. "Wouldn't you offer someone else compassion if they were in your situation?"

"Yeah." I sobbed while sitting in a chair across from him in his corner office with a mountain view. "But this was my fault."

"But it was an *accident*. You didn't intend to cut your thumb off," he tenderly reassured me.

I looked away. It was *my* fault. For whatever reason, some days I just can't give myself a break. I beat myself up and cast the blame so heavily onto my own shoulders that I can't find any peace from the situation—even over a year and a half later.

But I have been called the Queen of Avoidance, and I would definitely agree with that title. I put on my happy face and try my best to just act like everything is okay. I constantly search my mind for potential paths, answers, or clues for the next target at which I should aim, but sometimes, I just want to give up. I want to adhere to the negative thoughts that scream in my mind to surrender on this pursuit, to find dulling complacency and learn to like it.

"In order to tell your brain that your anxieties can't hurt you, you must invite them in. Sit with those thoughts and images that scare you, and let the uncomfortable feelings rise. Show yourself that they won't hurt you," Dr. T recited.

"But it's hard. I don't want to think about it," I replied stubbornly while taking deep breaths and trying to calm the overwhelming tension that had slowly crept up my calves since I had walked through the door.

Dr. T practiced what was referred to as "exposure technique." This is the process of exposing oneself to the very thoughts that induce fear and/or anxiety. I hated the constant reliving of my trauma, and I resented Dr. T for regularly prodding me to face my fears. For weeks on end, I would make my way down the winding hallway back to his corner office and take my usual seat in the blue armchair that sits facing the windows. On the small table to my right sat the now familiar image of the Dr. Seuss book titled *Oh, The Places You'll Go!* Once, when Dr. T stepped out to take an important phone call, I read it.

"You have brains in your head.
You have feet in your shoes.
You can steer yourself any direction you choose.
You're on your own.
And you know what you know.
And YOU are the one who'll decide where to go…"

Although I liked Dr. T, for the first six months or so, I really didn't believe his methods and tactics were helping me. I would get upset almost every visit because he would ask me to retell the same story over and over. Eventually, I told him I felt like I was just hitting the play button on a recording device, a similar feeling I'd felt when strangers and acquaintances would ask me what happened. In fact, it almost felt like it was not me telling the story. I would just sit back and say the same words I'd said many times before. Whimsical phrases would fall from my lips, and I would watch the reactions from onlookers as they would inspect my hand with awe and curiosity.

"Yup, the whole thing was on the ground," I'd often retort when my observer would ask how deep it was cut.

When I first started seeing Dr. T, I told myself I would be honest with him about everything I felt and thought. I needed to be 100 percent transparent. This is not something I did thoroughly with the previous psychologist I saw while still living in Ohio before I met Dr. T. I was not dishonest, nor did I lie to the previous doctor, but rather I would willingly not express dark feelings I had or talk about disturbing experiences of recurring images and fearful thoughts. Instead, I just wanted him to report that I was okay, that I was close to a full recovery. I did this so I could get on with my life and let this accident live in the past.

Boy, was that the wrong way to approach the situation. By burying deeper the hurt and dark truths that took residence in the dormant corners of my being, I actually, unknowingly, gave them great power over some of my belief systems. And even though Dr. T helped me to truly face these dark feelings, once I was back in Reno, they persistently haunted me.

I thought when I moved back home that I would start a new chapter, a new beginning. I expected change and anticipated difficulty, but the reality of this transition turned out to be much worse than I had thought. My road ended just when I thought it had merely begun. I hit a wall. I sank into a deeper depression, and rather than expressing that truth, I repressed it. I hid my feelings in the recesses of my heart and mind where they began to marinate, rot, and become concentrated truths I actually believed. This was not a good move emotionally.

Sixty-nine days after I pulled into Reno with my mom, dogs, and all of my possessions in tow, I found myself lying in my bathtub. The tepid water started to feel cold after being in there for hours, and I heavily considered taking action to end my life.

My biggest drive to stay alive was—and still is—the fact that I don't want others to give up hope. Somehow, I value the pulse in another's veins over my own—I'm still working on understanding this. I know if I opt out, then it sends the message that it's okay to *choose* to be done.

Although it is always an option, it only seems to be a way out because we believe death is the end of suffering. I mean, it has to be, right? But what if what we perceive about suicide is wrong, and we kill ourselves just to learn that the suffering continues? The notion that suffering ends with death is something that may provide the living with peace, but how can we know if it's true? We can't, I suppose. We can just choose what we believe. And I guess, somewhere deep down, I believe there is always hope, that things can change in this life, and that it's worth continuing to try to make those changes happen.

A few days after this experience, I turned to my dad, tearfully explaining what I had felt and thought of while in the bathtub that night. He was on his way to work, and I'd arrived at his house to watch my eleven-year-old half-brother for a few hours. My father had known his own battles with mental health, and he'd known the struggles I'd faced throughout my life as well.

"Well, kid, you can take your life, or you can take your life back," he encouraged in an empowering way that reminded me of the fighter that dwelled within me.

Having this kind of conversation reminded me that I am a survivor. So often in life, the going gets tough. I've known and witnessed this truth all too well. I'm not the type of person to wallow in self-pity, maybe for a day—okay, or a week—but I've always been solution-oriented and a problem solver.

It took over three weeks from the day I decided to change my attitude and perspective to get some results. During this time, I decided to find a psychologist in Reno. I needed a professional I could talk to about my mental unwellness, someone who I decided I would be completely transparent with—insert Dr. T. Finding Dr. T was not an easy process, but shifting doors of the maze I was in led me to sitting in his office just one month after that dreadful night in my bathtub.

The idea of committing to transparency was daunting because I felt utterly inadequate. Like, why are my feelings valid? How is my life that bad when there are millions suffering in much worse situations than mine? Eventually, I even found myself asking questions like, "What do I even have to offer?" I remember feeling like I didn't really have anything to give, but I still wanted to inspire hope. I still don't know if that's possible. I mean, can I be a giver of hope, yet have no proof? Nothing to show for it? I guess the proof is that I'm still here... and I'm writing this.

I can't tell you how many times I thought of ending my life. I even attempted to do it on two occasions when I was a teenager after suffering a dreadful head injury when I was a freshman in high school. But because I had come close to tragedy a number of times throughout my lifetime, I have learned that I actually value others' lives quite dearly. So why was it that I couldn't value my own?

Although I typically shoot for the stars, I knew even just some effort could get me to a healthy middle ground, get me even. I've always been able to mirror what I see around me, so I decided to take that approach to get my life from the low I was in to at least a state of feeling average. Many people can relate to the lack of challenges that surround them, and they happily seek their own pleasures of finding or creating happiness within. So why couldn't I do that? I had been acting like I couldn't meet myself in mediocrity, so instead I had been backsliding, giving in to the lure of depression and contemplating commitment.

The truth is, I've never been the commitment type, and I know that about myself. My short attention span will be excited and enthralled for a good run, but then, I'll be right back in the lap of dissatisfaction. It's like I'm constantly telling Santa what I want this week rather than this year. I was frustrated with myself for having this quirk, and a fearful stream of questions consumed me. *Will I always be so impermanent? Will I ever give myself the necessary time to actually become? Or will the lack of patience consume me and keep pushing me to go somewhere new, to try something different, to be someone else for a time?* Though I was focused on the negative aspects of this trait, I realize now this actually proved to be a blessing in regard to the idea I had been weighing.

Did I mention I'm good at concealing these feelings? You wouldn't know it if you just met me or if you saw pictures of me. I'm good at displaying happiness and light. And don't get me wrong, I am joyful and love to share smiles, laughter, and inside jokes, but, just as we all do, I have another side to me, one that not very many people see. Even the people closest to me *rarely* see the dark side, the sad side, the antagonist who dwells within me, who belittles and doubts my every move. I'd say an evil voice (if you will) lives in all of us; we just don't see it in some as much as we see it in others.

At the same time I decided to seek professional mental help, I had also decided to look for a real job. I'd spent months in the workers' compensation system I was part of, which provided the needs for the first year of recovery. It had helped me tremendously, but with no more apparent results coming from that angle, I decided to embrace the go-getter I once knew to help me plug back into the real world. Yes, I wanted to earn money, but I also wanted regular interaction with people; I wanted to find a routine and have some sort of structure for the short-term vision of my future. At that particular point, I had nothing in mind for the coming months—nothing to look forward to, nothing to talk about, and certainly nothing to focus my energy and efforts on.

I needed change, and when I originally decided to move home from Ohio, I had thought simply moving back would be enough, but it wasn't. I realized if I was really going to put my injury in the past, it was going to take more than just surrounding myself in the familiarity of my hometown. It's true that there's no place like home—Ohio taught me that—but I was learning that coming "home" meant more than just a physical shift; it was something you had to do emotionally too.

Home

It's hard to believe that I lived in Ohio for two and a half years. Looking back, I couldn't have dreamt of a more perfect adventure. Within each and every trying circumstance, there was collateral beauty; there was always hope. I had some really low and difficult moments: from finding myself half naked in a Starbucks both clueless and sober, to being covered head to toe in poison ivy from a systemic reaction to a skin disease I'd never known to be so evil, to lying in an ambulance with the emergency medical responder holding one of my appendages in a bag separate from my body. But I also experienced some magical moments of coincidence and serendipitous joy, such as having the opportunity to sit near and share conversation with an admirable woman, Temple Grandin, on an airplane flight from Columbus to Denver; holding hands in the warmth of the sunshine in reunion and forgiveness with a friend from an excruciatingly challenging and sticky situation; and remarkably recovering with 100 percent feeling and a highly functioning capacity from the amputation of my thumb. Seeing my doctor's pride and hearing his positive reaction for both his team's performance as well as my efforts toward the rehabilitation of this replant flooded my heart with joy.

There were certainly moments when I thought I'd never reach some of the milestones I eventually conquered, but having encouragement, a team of support, and the will to recover carried me through difficult times. At just the right moments, I would receive words of affirmation, witness physical progress, experience emotional empowerment, engage in opportune distractions, and reach and break through barriers of illusion and defeat. Journeys are a process, and that process is made up of tedious efforts and consistent practices of hope and discipline. There are unique systems and procedures for healing, growth, and success, and at twenty-nine, I am just beginning to understand the importance of each of these.

I am so thankful I had support each and every day from the moment my hand was maimed by the bandsaw. I needed my people, my advocates; they were essential in my healing. I find myself now slipping into that role with others, as I'm committed to help anyone through the recovery process that comes after trauma, even if it's just to help calm their nerves in relation to the anxiety and uncertainty that can come with an unexpected, life-altering injury. Any injury can be debilitating for a while, and sudden trauma can cause incredible emotional angst. I would say, as I've learned, it's very important to lean on your support team throughout the entirety of the healing process. Luckily for me, I had a boatload of aid from the DWC, consolation from my friends who I met from the farm in Lima, encouragement from coworkers and acquaintances from the steakhouse, and comfort from various people in between who I met while working at the pub and through other differing encounters. I spent regular hours on the phone and FaceTime with my loved ones back home, and I even found inspiration from unknown strangers I encountered along the way. I found solace in a vast array of people. I was not without help for a second during my ordeal, but it was up to me to reach out and seek these pillars in times of despair. Although there were moments when I felt terribly alone and lost in the agonizing unknown of how this ordeal would play out, I learned those were the times especially that I needed to actively plug into all realms of care available to me.

Lately, I've realized that having a solid foundation of support is a crucial factor in wellness. Whether it is for emotional, physical, mental, or spiritual well-being, we all need some type of group, team, tribe, or community to help us get through the difficulties we are guaranteed to face. For many people, a family can provide this backing. For others, it's a solid group of friends; even a steady work atmosphere can provide the necessary comfort for an individual. Oftentimes, it is a combination of all and/or even other means, but regardless of what it looks like, support is a crucial ingredient for overall wellness. And if you're lucky, like I know I was, means of care can be spread across many locations.

The catch with having support in multiple places though is that usually means you have to say goodbye, which is never easy. It's not easy to look into the eyes of loved ones and never know if you will see them again. When I moved to Ohio, I had no idea I would develop the strong relationships and connections I did, and I'm so grateful for those, but that just made my ultimate departure even harder. With the news that I would be back for surgery, I was relieved to know I would get to see these familiar faces again.

When I embarked on my journey to Ohio, I sought adventure, connection, experience, and growth. And though for some time my mind was wrapped up in my injury, I can see now that I achieved all of these things and then some! I developed into a woman I didn't imagine I could be, and I learned the language of my soul and how to understand the desires of my heart like never before. I am courageous and fearless in ways I still don't fully understand, but after getting a glimpse of these traits, I realized I want to continue to test and utilize these strengths while I can feel them coursing passionately through my bloodstream. Tomorrow is not a guarantee, and as I've observed, life can drastically change in an instant.

On my second to last visit to Ohio, in April of 2018, I met my old bowling buddy Cliff for a light game of disc golf at Alum Creek Lake. This was another one-handed pastime I discovered during my recovery. We played a quick round and enjoyed the weather and each other's company before finding a cozy bench perched on the water's edge to rest our feet and sink into conversation.

"So, have you been working in Reno?" he asked.

"Yeah, I got another job at a steakhouse," I admitted. "But I'm on medical leave again for now for this surgery. This process with workers' comp has been a nightmare," I explained to Cliff. "I was supposed to be in vocational rehab when I moved back to Reno, but that never happened."

"What's vocational rehab?" he inquired.

"Well, since my doctor originally recommended that I do not go back to meat cutting due to the long-term effects of my injury, workers' comp offered a vocational rehab program that would help get me into a new career."

"Oh, okay. Cool. So, what new career are you going to do?"

"Well, that's just the thing. I enrolled in the program and did all the initial placement testing. I even found a company to help me in Reno so when I moved home I could get started, but as soon as the doctor said I needed another surgery, workers' comp said I didn't qualify for vocational rehab since I was not 'medically stable.'"

"Well, that sounds like a bummer," Cliff said sympathetically. "So, what exactly happened?"

"Oh my God, it was hellish and horrible for a few months. It took workers' comp three months to approve the condition the doctor needed in order to seek approval for the surgery. Then, I needed an MRI to pinpoint the exact problem in my hand, and it took another three months to get *that* approved and performed. Until the surgery was actually scheduled, they wouldn't give me any financial support. In the meantime, I decided to get a job at a steakhouse, and I just didn't fully disclose all the details to my boss about my hand injury. I also hired a lawyer. When he spoke to the insurance company, they told him I must have 'fallen through the cracks.'" I felt my annoyance bubble as I relived some of the details of the past six months.

"Shit… So, you just had surgery, and you said it went well. Does that mean things are getting better now?" he inquired.

"Not really. I mean, I guess things are actually happening, but I have to fly back in a couple weeks to have another surgery. Since I started working again, the pain in my thumb has become unbearable, so I just came back to get the hardware taken out of my thumb. I already feel relief." I held my thumb with my right hand and continued, "Apparently, the MRI I had done in Reno was the wrong test, and it didn't get the doctor the results he needed to pinpoint the problem with my blood flow. I had to cry on the phone to the insurance adjuster to get another approval to have *another* MRI done by a radiologist here in Columbus. I guess my surgeon works with him all the time, so we'll see." I sighed.

Cliff just listened as we stared out across the water.

"They said they'll call me with the results and schedule another surgery soon. The kicker is my doctor said he's taking a sabbatical in June, so I need to come back as soon as possible. If it all works out, I'll be back in less than a month. My doctor originally wanted to perform both surgeries at the same time, but since I 'fell through the cracks' and was in so much pain, it has now become another drawn-out process. I just hope the end is near and the results are worth it. I do already feel better having the metal gone, so I guess that's a positive."

"Do you think you will go back to the steakhouse?" Cliff asked.

"I guess, yeah. Probably after the other surgery. My boss is really cool and said he will keep my position for me."

"Do you want to go back to butchery?"

"Yeah, maybe one day. I certainly can't do the job now, but I've been doing some research in Reno, trying to meet some local beef farmers and butchers to see what potential there is," I told him. "But for now, I just want to be done with this chapter in my life. I want to be out of the workers' comp system, and just done with it all. I will live with whatever I have to, but I am sick of letting other people dictate how my life goes."

"Are you going to try for the vocational rehab again?" Cliff asked.

"Haha!" I laughed. "Hell no. When I'm done and my doctor gives me the thumbs up, I'm done with all of this bullshit. I feel like my life has been dangling on a string in front of me, and every time I am hopeful that I can reach the next phase, it escapes my grasps."

"That sounds frustrating," he empathized. "I hope it all works out for you and your thumb. You two have certainly been through a lot," Cliff stated as he glanced down at my bandaged hand.

"Yeah, me too." I sighed. "Thanks."

We sat quietly for a bit and exchanged our usual hopeful and imagination-filled dreams of the future before we walked back to the parking lot.

Within three weeks, I was on an airplane flying back to Ohio to have another surgery, my mom accompanying me. This time, the surgeon worked on my artery in an attempt to increase the blood flow to my thumb. Afterward, my mom played nurse as we spent a few days laid up in a hotel room near the surgery center. I was in much more pain than the minor surgery a few weeks prior, so I literally spent most of those days of recovery sleeping and being taken care of by my Ohio family after my mom left.

"Your capillary refill is faster than in your other fingers," the surgeon proudly informed me when I saw him for my ten-day follow-up.

We were both extremely happy with the results. He let me know it would gradually get better as well once the scar tissue healed. I had now reached a bittersweet moment with him. The gratitude I felt and admiration for this man was beyond words. He encouraged me that my will to succeed played an eighty percent role in this process, and he referred to me as his "star patient."

"You know, some people get so down on themselves about their situation that they lose the will to push for the best results. I can only do so much; medicine, science, and technology can only go so far, and if the patient doesn't want to fight to get optimal results, their chances for complete recovery lessen," Dr. Wozniak told me. "It's been a pleasure to work with you, Karissa. Your attitude and commitment to recovery have been a powerful catalyst in this process. Keep aiming high."

These words warmed my heart as I recalled some grueling, painful, and hopeless times. I was so impressed with this man. It was obvious that he was in love with his profession as a hand microsurgeon, and his skills undoubtedly spoke for themselves. He was a master of his craft, and I admired that.

When it got time for me to say goodbye this time, I knew it would be awhile before I returned to Ohio. I wanted to make my rounds and spend some quality time with those I would miss. I felt a tremendous torrent of love and support. Although I made sure to focus on prioritizing my healing, it wasn't easy to spend my time resting, knowing I may not see some of these dear souls again.

But of course, it wouldn't be a trip to Ohio without a little side excursion, and this time it was sweet Claire who proposed the plan when she called me to see how I was recovering from surgery. She listened with compassion as I explained to her the final process, and she offered to put me up for some R and R, Claire style. I didn't hesitate to drive straight to her house. When I arrived, she told me she would be leaving in a few days for a vacation on the shores of North Carolina. She'd rented a huge house and planned for a week on the beach, with craft-filled days and catching up on some z's. While I was sitting in her kitchen, slightly doped up from the painkillers, she received a phone call. It was her sister-in-law, calling to inform Claire that their family couldn't make the trip. She was distraught; it was too late to cancel the house, and she'd already promised her daughter a beach getaway.

"You wouldn't be interested in changing your flight and joining us on the coast, would you?" she asked in jest.

"Do you know who you're talking to?" I smiled while I calculated in my head my agenda for the next few days. "I think I could swing that," I retorted.

"Oh my gosh, really? I was only half serious. But you know, a relaxing beachfront vacation is probably a prescription your doctor would write. I mean, you won't have to lift a finger—and definitely not a thumb. You know my Emily would be so stoked if you could join us! Hell, that would be the best vacation ever!"

So it was decided. I made the necessary adjustments to my agenda, and we hit the open road. Claire's niece still joined us on the vacation, and Claire had also invited another dear friend along as well. That intimate time with four lovely ladies proved to be the perfect remedy after the trials of the past year and a half. We strolled the sandy beaches just north of the Outer Banks. We bonded over tearful conversations of the struggles that life seemingly always presents. We dined like queens both out at local restaurants and on homecooked meals made in our cozy cottage. Claire had packed every possible art supply she had, so we painted seashells, colored mandalas, and spent hours relieving our woes in creative artistic fashion. It was on this trip that I was reminded of the important nourishments necessary for our souls. The ocean, comradery, and self-reflection surely helped.

By the time I flew back to Nevada, my energy was low but my spirits were high. I spent the summer recuperating, getting back into the swing of things at the steakhouse in Reno and proudly showing off the incredible recovery of my once-amputated thumb. I had found my new normal, and I felt okay settling into my life as a career waitress. A small part of me still missed the excitement of butchery, the finesse it took to move a blade through thick slabs of meat and fat, but for now, I was perfectly content to just *be*. I practiced acceptance and let go of expectations. And it wasn't long before I could see a tiny new sprig of life rise up from the roots I'd planted when I moved back home.

Closure

2018 brought me perspective.

The trials I endured and the adventures therein led me to have clarity, peace, and closure, but it wasn't until I ruthlessly faced my fears, pursued my heart's soft whispers, and decided to live my life with acceptance and fearless abandon that I finally found myself moving on from the girl I was to the woman I wanted to become. In my efforts to seek a valued life, I allowed it to find me. I let this powerful force breakthrough walls of insecurity and doubt, and with great introspection and bravery, I was able to witness the raw, unadulterated Karissa.

While perusing Instagram one day, I came across an advertisement for a retreat hosted by two of my favorite authors: Elizabeth Gilbert, who wrote the world-renowned book, *Eat, Pray, Love,* and Cheryl Strayed, whose most famous work was *Wild,* a memoir about her journey through personal trials and a solo quest along the Pacific Crest Trail. The retreat was titled, "Brave Magic: An Invitation to Curiosity, Creativity and Courage." This sounded right up my alley, and I spent a good half hour or so researching the event. Then and there, I booked my reservation. It was to be held in late September 2018, at a facility tucked in the California Redwoods, which was about a five-hour drive from Reno. The cost of the retreat included housing, three meals a day, and a variety of wellness activities, such as yoga, Tai Chi, guided meditation, and mild outdoor excursions. I couldn't wait to go.

Before I get to that, I should probably back up for a second. See, a few months prior to my soul-cleansing retreat, I had received an email informing me that the next gathering of the Butcher's Manifesto would be held in Berlin, Germany, during the first week of October. Although the idea of making the scene with my favorite meat enthusiasts appealed to me, I really didn't think too much of it at first—though the announcement did incline me to reach out to Carmen, who I'd lost touch with during the distracting trials over the past year. She replied rather promptly and extended an invitation to come check out their operation if I was going to be in Germany for the manifesto. She told me they still had an empty apartment and would love to offer me work and accommodations for a season, if I was interested. If anything, she encouraged me to just come for a visit. I didn't hesitate to take her up on her offer as I no longer could bury the feeling that my meat-loving aspirations felt unresolved. I couldn't pass up this opportunity; it was just too perfect.

Before I knew it, Carmen and I were exchanging details about timelines, travel arrangements, and plans for my coming to Bavaria. She gave me tips about trains and cheap flights and assured me they were just as excited to have me come to Untergriesbach, the small town where she lived, as I was for the opportunity. As my excitement grew, I let myself dream again. *Maybe I'll move to Germany to work as a butcher and learn to be as precise and elegant with a blade like Hans is,* I thought. The idea of restoring my dormant passion flooded my thoughts with wild dreams and possibilities. I felt like this door had been previously nailed shut and barricaded, but now, I was ready to bust through in dynamite fashion.

I had a whirlwind of a three weeks between mid-September and the beginning of October. I drove myself wide-eyed and thirsty for inspiration to the retreat in California. I spent three brief days delving into my soul, once again, and surrendering to the unknown. To be honest, I thought much of the time would be spent writing, talking about writing, or hearing the stories of what led these women to be authors, but it was so much more than that. The weekend did contain some writing activities, but they were self-guided, thought-provoking exercises that really challenged us to look within for answers about painful truths, personal setbacks, and hidden desires, as well as producing and sharing contemplative tidbits that were completely individualized. I made some impactful connections with a few special souls who inspired me to be realistic and vulnerable. What I got most out of my time was reassurance and permission to be myself, just as I was: a little broken, a little badass, a little ambitious, and a little reserved. These realizations set the tone perfectly for my next big feat. I was ready.

Nine days later, I was in Europe. It goes without saying, I had a bumpy start to my trip, but what the hell. I live for this shit!

And what do we do when we're on the journey of a lifetime and want to share it?

We post about it on Facebook.

I acknowledge that I am not a great picture-taker… but I do think I am a pretty good adventure-taker and storyteller, so I will do my best to share fun bits of this adventure!

Part A: "Difference Maker."

Saturday, I set off to travel to Germany. My dear, sweet friend drove me to California in order for me to have a direct, nonstop flight overseas. With much anticipation, I arrived at the airport four hours prior to my flight, just to be safe.

Lo and behold, my flight was delayed. First, a half hour. Then, an hour and a half, then five hours, then nineteen hours… and eventually twenty-four hours.

The gate was filled with anxious travelers, quite a few who were headed to set sail on a three-week cruise out of Europe.

I felt badly for these passengers as they tried to scramble and figure out how to best navigate the situation. I remained relatively at ease and focused on trying to update my iPhone. (Why this is such a difficult task for me is a mystery.)

As you can imagine, once the final announcement was made that the flight would not leave that evening, semi-chaos ensued. Some 150+ passengers were now redirected to the nearest hotels and then in lines for vouchers, assistance, check-ins, Ubers, and taxis. I myself waited for the crowd to dissipate before I made any moves from the seat I had occupied pretty consistently for the previous ten hours. I felt as if I was not in a hurry for much at that point.

I decided to forego the line at the ticket counter and instead head to the taxi line and figure out my next move from there. I called the nearest eight or so hotels, all of whom informed me they were booked for the night. By the time I made it to be next up for a taxi, I changed my game plan to stay a little farther from the airport in order for the sweet voice on the other end of the line to bless my ears with the words, "Yes, we have a room available."

Just as the cab driver got out to help me load my bag, I heard the pleasant affirmation from the conversation via my AirPods and swiftly gave the cabby the address of the hotel. "Only about fifteen minutes away," the cab driver reassured me when I asked if it was a far drive.

I checked in and asked if many people had called due to the flight delay, and the friendly staff replied, "Not really."

I walked to my room, tired but happy that I had somewhere to rest before doing it all again the next day. At this point, the flight was due to leave at 1:00 p.m., so with encouragement from my support team, I figured I would just make the best of it and head to the airport again tomorrow. When I got to my small apartment of a room, which the hotel described as a "suite," I was not too thrilled about the stains that covered the carpet and drapes. The hotel itself was certainly old. The furniture and box television sets supported the fact that this place could use an update—or seven. This suite had a full-on kitchen, living room, two hallways, a back patio with sliding door, and a separate bathroom and bedroom. I briefly looked throughout the place, in cabinets, under the bed and couches and then made sure the windows and doors all locked. I was a little hesitant to climb into my bed, wondering if the sheets were actually clean. But I was tired, and frankly, I've slept in much worse places, so I didn't really care. I figured I would just wash it all off the next day with a shower.

In the morning, I stumbled down to the "continental breakfast," which was literally a few donuts and a large box of Honey Bunches of Oats with Almonds (which actually happens to be my favorite cereal, so that was a plus!) I grabbed a cup of coffee and a paper bowl of cereal and walked back to my apartment to sit at my dining table (literally) and get my bearings for the day. It was about 9:00 a.m. by now, and I had already received notice that my 1:00 p.m. flight was pushed back again until 6:00 p.m. What the heck am I going to do with myself today? *I wondered just before I called to ask for a later checkout. "Sorry, but we can only give you one hour extra. You can check out at noon."*

After doing some quick math and Google Mapping to find just where I was in relation to the airport, I noticed I wasn't far from a water source, so I decided to put my running shoes on and go for a morning jaunt. BEST IDEA EVER! I made it to the shorefront with a gorgeous view of the city of San Francisco and enjoyed a nice run on the beach. I even found myself having a great conversation with a fellow runner who was wearing a Tough Mudder shirt. (An event I've participated in three times and love to hear stories from other participants). He gave me a tip about where to run and ideas to help occupy myself for the day as he informed me

249

there was a mall nearby to where we stood.

After a quick shower and checkout, I strolled over to the mall, luggage in tote, and wandered a bit before landing in a nail salon. A pedicure sounds nice, *I thought to myself, and the gracious ladies let me sit in the massage chair for about an hour, even after my amazing toe treatment was finished. While sitting there getting my feet rubbed, I met a woman who I shared my story with, and she asked where I was planning to eat lunch. She then recommended the "best burger in town" and encouraged me that it was a short half-mile walk and worth every step. I took her advice, and after my mini spa experience, I headed over to devour what was a delicious, homemade, locally sourced burger. It was smothered with peanut butter and bacon, and my taste buds were in heaven. My appetite was satiated when I left for the airport—this time only two hours early.*

I now sit preparing to leave my hotel room just outside of Berlin, Germany, and I will make my way down to the southern part of the country to meet up with my generous hosts! With anticipation for the next leg of my trip, I can't help but already feel a deep satisfaction for the journey. I have quite a way to go, and I am breathing in and soaking up each glorious step. I am thankful and full of joy and peace, despite the hiccups. I know the next week will be more than I could imagine!

I look forward to being in the foothills of the Alps for a time and experiencing life just a little bit different than what I am used to. The thrill of the unknown fuels my curiosity, and the incredible journey of meeting people, charting unfamiliar territory, making precious connections, and stepping away from my comfort zone fulfills a hunger that resides deep within… if only for a brief time. (Obviously, my wanderlust nature keeps beckoning me onward, upward, outward, and inward.) Until next time. **XOXO**

I had just over a week to investigate all the potential opportunities I could find for my future. It was like someone had handed me a perfectly wrapped gift, and inside was everything I hadn't let myself want while I was recovering. I couldn't believe I was again meeting the people who had invited me across the world to stay with them. It was magical. I was staying with an ardent family of butchers who had developed quite an impressive brand in their region over a few generations. They were welcoming and warm, intelligent, and truly German made. I spoke no German, despite the idea I once owned that I would learn the language before I traveled to stay with them. We did our best to communicate, once again relying on technology and Wi-Fi to bridge the gaps. We toured their facilities, and I was beyond impressed. State-of-the-art equipment welcomed us into the palace of a processing house. Our shoes and hands were sanitized by walking over a device that looked like it was made for a spaceship. Equipped with rolling brushes and bright green lights, I felt a little unease as I followed the girls ahead of me and mimicked their moves. It just so happened that when I arrived, after a seven-hour drive from Berlin to Bavaria, Carmen was hosting a tour of the facilities for a group of girls who were all her employees in the various meat markets in the region. It was the perfect start to this trip, and I was happy to learn that a few of them spoke broken English, so I stayed close to them during the tour.

Carmen welcomed me into her home where she lived with her three young children and fellow butcher better half, Christoph. Luckily, he too spoke enough English for us to not have *every* conversation via Google Translate. The kids spoke zero English, but they insisted that I understood them when they spoke to me. It was a joyous surprise to spend time with those little ones, because really, you don't need to speak the same language to frolic and play and laugh. Her daughter brushed my hair and painted my nails while her oldest son whirled around the table, making sure I had a drink, some silverware, and a napkin at mealtimes.

The group took me to a few of their butcher shops that were in relatively close driving distances as well as to a beer festival where we met up with an American friend. I was relieved when I no longer had to struggle to have a conversation, and he gladly filled me in on the history and intricacies of the little country villages of Bayern, which is what Germans call Bavaria—weird, right? They also took me to a scenic overlook on the boarder of Germany and Austria. We only went to one local eatery since we mostly ate their tasty sausages, but we often drank beer.

It was a whirlwind adventure, and I couldn't have asked for better hosts. I was jet-lagged and exhausted, but I didn't want to miss a thing. I was sad to leave, but for some reason, I felt that I would see them again.

To my surprise, on my last day, Hans and Carmen set me up with a whole box of sausage varieties and an official Heindl apron so I could share their craftsmanship and represent their brand at the Butcher's Manifesto, which was coming up quick!

The second part of my trip to Germany was spent in Berlin, a romantic and dreamlike city. Butcher's Manifesto had organized a butchery booth filled with live demonstrations of whole animal butchery, start-to-finish sausage making, and an array of informative interview panels at the Stadt Land Food Festival. The theme of the festival was "Better food for all," and our booth proclaimed, "Better meat for all." I quickly rekindled relationships with some of the familiar faces I'd met the previous year in Copenhagen. I dove in to any and all work that needed to be done, hanging fliers, setting up tables, unpacking vehicles, food prep, and more. I was riding the wave of the past two weeks of revitalizing my spirit, and I wasn't about to hold back. By now, I was also more inspired to share the story of my injury and the transitions I underwent throughout my recovery. I mean, all of it had led me to be exactly where I was... in freaking Berlin!

"Where do you see yourself in ten years in the industry?" a group of us was asked during a female butcher panel.

My reply even shocked me, "As some of you know, I suffered a great injury that hindered my pursuit of being a butcher. I have not since returned to the field, but I now see the potential for my role as a voice in the meat industry. In ten years, I hope to be leading conversations and building connections within our industry. I hope to spend my time discovering the needs of different people, from producers to consumers, in order to develop quality partnerships across the board."

Hearing myself say out loud that I was basically done with the physical side of tedious butchery was a breakthrough I had yet to acknowledge and truly believe. I thought this trip would reinstate my role in the craft and besiege my future with meat cleaving opportunities. But I realized something else: I wanted to lay this dream to rest. I no longer felt the need to prove anything, to anyone, not even myself. I was at peace with the cycle that had run its course.

During this trip, I realized that, although I still had great love for food and desired to be a positive influence in the food industry, I did not need to identify my career as a butcher in order to overcome the fears and insecurities that had grown within me since my injury. These were separate issues. I suppose I had known somewhere, deep down, that I was done with the pursuit of returning to the bandsaw professionally, but it wasn't until I spoke the words aloud and made the decision to be done with that pursuit that I finally experienced closure.

It took twenty-two months, four surgeries, and two trips overseas for me to feel undefeated by the traumatic event that altered the course of my life. For so long, I believed I was a victim to this accident. I allowed myself to trudge through depression, with anxiety and helplessness in tote. I let falsehoods and setbacks of being injured hinder my heart's pursuit of happiness and dreams of living a life I valued. I spent so much time thinking I needed to return to butchery in order to prove something. What I ended up discovering instead was a truth I had known and believed all along: I am a writer.

I had set out to write a book when I first moved to Ohio. I originally wanted to document the story and adventures therein. So when my injury occurred, it was natural for me and cathartic to record my recovery. A wise person once told me, "Every writer needs a story." And, as it turned out, I now had a story to tell. My story is one of healing and growth, of learning to love yourself, of taking risks and pursuing adventure.

I can honestly say that the plot twists and events that unfolded in the past few years have led me to see myself in a beautiful new light. I confidently embrace the gifts and talents that align my heart and my circumstances. Instead of seeking to prove something or perform in a certain way, I now focus on feeding my hungry spirit and eagerly sharing the love and light that dwell within me. My dream is to be a positive influence, to inspire others to engage in a life that is exclusively fulfilling to them. I hope to encourage others to overcome the disheartening beliefs that stand in the way of living their own unique life to the fullest. I can honestly say, from my multiple experiences on the matter: Starting over is not easy, but it is certainly worth it.

Acknowledgments

I am so thankful for the journey of writing this book. The story was more than life-altering for me, it was life-defining. For so long, I never thought I could identify myself as a writer. I thought being a writer meant having some literary degree or having a magazine publish your work or working as a person who writes words professionally. I'm just a girl who loves to write in her journal, hell, who *needs* to write in her journal. I have evidence of having kept a diary since I was eleven years old. And in the past two decades, I have only grown in my love affair to document my feelings and contemplate my life via pen and pad. Thankfully this practice led me to forge a tellable story from the difficult challenges I lived. Now that I own being a writer as one of my many identities, I feel a peace within me that surely will grow. And that peace carries deep gratitude for the people who helped me get to this point.

My mother, my mother, my mother, my mom, my mama, mi madre. Without this woman, I'm not sure where I would be. First of all, I am so much like her as far as having a "get 'er done" attitude, so thanks to mom; we got 'er done. She has certainly been my biggest cheerleader and truest confidant for my whole life, but without her in my corner, my story would be quite different. Thank you, mom, for encouraging me, listening to me and pushing me forward each step of the way.

My dear father, another important person in my inner circle. I've always been a daddy's girl and I'm thankful for the man my father is and the daughter he raised. Throughout my life, he has spoiled me with love, wisdom and patience. He is the one person who encouraged me to read books and constantly try to be better today than I was yesterday. Thank you, dad. "You raise me up to more than I can be."

To all the people in this story, you became my family. You helped me uncover hidden parts of my being; and I didn't necessarily know it at the time, but your acceptance, support and love stimulated the life in my veins. With shared conversation and experience, I grew to understand just a little bit more what it means to be ferociously alive.

To my three brothers, Dutney, Roger and Rory Jr. I'm thankful for each of our unique relationships. Dutney, you are one of a kind and everyone who knows you knows that. Roger, you've always proven to be caring and loving, even when you flex your muscles. And Rory Jr., my monkey, you are so independent and loving, you inspire me and comfort me with your sweet presence. And Suzie, my amazing, smart, love-filled stepmom, your influence in my life from those trying teenage years into womanhood has been priceless to me. You are a gem and your spirit is radiant and contagious.

To all of my friends, extended family and mere acquaintances who flooded me with connection, insight and kindness, I wish I could name you all here, but specifically my life has been forever impacted by Charlotte Nordman, Mel Rems, Tina Gavin, Jill Defreitas, Chase Crowley, Nicole Martinkus, Michelle Phillips, the Kvam family, Linda and Lindsay Chapman, Adam Hoppe, Craig Cochran, the Trainwreck family, the whole S & W gang, and every Simon that has ever lived.

I am so thankful for my editors at Polished It, Anna and Lindsay. You ladies gave me advice and insight that allowed my story to be as polished as its gonna get!

A huge thanks to the Bareknuckle Brand crew in Reno for helping me to get focused on the road to self-publishing. Your creativity and professionalism elevated me at just the right time.

It saddens me to mention the dear loved ones I've lost since the initial writing of this book:

Frank Gibson Sr., who raised an incredible family and welcomed me into his world without hesitation. My time with you will live in a precious place in my heart forever.

After battling cancer for a time and taken much too soon, David Auger, may you rest in peace.

My little Tater Tot, the best friend and road-dog a girl could ask for. You brought me home and helped me live a life filled with love and adventure, gentle Tato-kisses, and lots and lots of water.

Made in the USA
Columbia, SC
10 January 2020